STRANGER
IN MY
WORLD

By Margaret Nogan

© 2017 Margaret Nogan

Printed in the United States of America.

CONTENTS

To Chris

Always

Margaret Rogan

DEDICATION

This book is dedicated to my two children,
Catherine Thurstlic and William Nogan.

FORWARD

I have watched him dream by a quiet stream
I have seen the loneliness in his eyes
I have felt the warmth that dwells within
This stranger that I love.
What is it that he is thinking,
That make the shadows start.
Why are the furrows in his brow?
Each one tears at my heart
I pray success will ease his sorrow
And bring a smile to his face.
I hope someday, this love I feel
Can fill that lonely, aching place
LEFT THERE BY SOMEONE ELSE.

I

Linda O' Connor sat at her desk in the quiet news office. She was busy typing up tomorrow's schedule for her daily column. She had been to see a new singer by the name of Rick Morrow a couple of nights before, and now she had decided to do an article about him.

As her thoughts went back to that night, a tiny sigh escaped from her parted lips. She remembered that, as she watched him perform, it seemed as though he was singing just for her. His green eyes teased until she could feel herself starting to blush.

"Strange how often I've thought of him since that night," her thoughts ran on.

Linda was so lost in her daydream everything else was forgotten. She did not hear the door, marked *Editor*, when it opened; nor did she notice the white-haired man when he stepped out into the outer office.

"Miss O'Connor, if you could spare the time, I would like to speak to you." His voice crackled in air like a whip.

Linda jumped to her feet.

"Yes, Mr. Weston, I will be right there," she stammered in confusion, all the while wondering how many times he had called her name before she answered him.

She hurried in to his office and carefully closed the door. When he spoke, his voice was gentle, and he showed no sign of his earlier gruffness.

"Sit down, Linda. I have something to ask you," he said, pointing to a chair by his desk.

Linda sat down and waited for him to continue. His next words stunned her.

"We have an interview lined up with Rick Morrow sometime this week and I think you would be the right one to cover it."

He gestured toward the door saying, "I think it might do you good to have something else to think about besides that column of yours for a few days."

Linda could feel the color rising in her cheeks. She wondered if he would feel the same if he knew what she'd been thinking.

She paused and then said, "All right, Mr. Weston, I would love to handle the interview. Where do I go? And when?"

Mr. Weston explained that the interview was to be held at Rick Morrow's apartment the following evening. There would be a cocktail party. Morrow had promised to give her time during the evening for an interview.

She hadn't counted on a social event and now she sat trying to think of a way out. She was sorry already that she had promised so quickly.

Mr. Weston broke into her thoughts saying, "Take tomorrow off, Linda. Sandy can cover for you here."

Thanking him, Linda opened the door and walked back to her desk, still in a daze. This had come to her so fast!

The office was empty by now and, looking at the clock, Linda saw it was after five. She covered her typewriter and walked out to the elevator that would carry her to the street below.

The evening was cold, and Linda pulled her camel hair coat closer around her as she headed for her car.

Driving through the evening traffic automatically, Linda's mind was still on Rick Morrow. Strange, she thought, how deep an impression he had made on her in such a short time.

Although the tempo of his show had carried a happy theme, a few times it seemed to Linda as though he must have felt very alone up there. She giggled at the thought of him being lonely. The stage was so crowded with women that, at the end of his performance, there was not an inch of the floor showing. No, she was sure he would never have to be alone.

Her little sports car purred along the freeway with no effort. Her car was a great source of pride to Linda. She had waited a long time before choosing it. It certainly made the long trips to Connecticut seem easier.

Linda had been born in Connecticut on an estate that was both beautiful and gracious. Her life there had been quiet and *dull*! That was why she had come to New York to live. At first, the noise of the big city had frightened her, and she felt as though she could never become a part of the fast-paced life. She smiled as she thought how quickly she had become used to the hectic, mad world that made up the city.

"Home at last," she sighed, pulling her sleek little car into the apartment garage. She stepped into the elevator and soon was standing in front of her own door. Turning the key in the lock, Linda pushed the door open and stepped into her tiny apartment. She loved her cozy place, perched high above the noise of the street. She had spent months decorating and buying furniture. Each chair and table had been selected with great care. The kitchen was bright and cheerful and, of course, her favorite color – yellow – predominated.

Linda stood by the sink washing lettuce for a salad. As she mechanically performed these tasks, her mind was busy thinking ahead to her interview with Rick Morrow.

She didn't feel very hungry, but It was no wonder when she considered the bubbly feeling she felt in her stomach every time she let her mind wander too far ahead. She finished dinner and washed the few dishes. As soon as the kitchen was cleaned to her satisfaction, Linda went into her bathroom and ran a bath scented with a delicious smelling fragrance. She hoped a nice warm bath would help her to relax and settle down a little.

Even as she entered her bedroom, her mind refused to do her bidding. Her thoughts kept straying back to Rick, even though she hardly knew him and had only seen him perform the one time.

"Oh, Linda," she scolded herself, "You are acting like a starry-eyed school girl instead of a mature reporter!"

Feeling thoroughly disgusted with herself, Linda turned out the light and went to bed. Oddly enough, it didn't take her long to fall asleep but, when she did, it was only to dream of Rick. She could see him standing on the stage, just as he had been that first time she had seen him. He looked so lonely standing there, and he was reaching out for someone. Was It her? Linda tried to call out to him. Her own cry woke her. Sitting up in bed, she turned on the lamp by her bedside. Her small alarm clock pointed to the hour of four. Touching her cheek, she could feel the wetness from her tears. Linda got out of bed and went to the kitchen. She sat there, drinking coffee until the gray dawn turned into a new day.

"Why...why?" Her mind kept repeating the question. "Why is this happening to me? Why did I dream such a troubled dream?"

Slowly Linda walked back to the bedroom and, closing the blinds on the early morning light, the troubled girl went back to sleep.

This time as she slept, a smile curved the corners of her pretty mouth. There were no more nightmares now – just deep, sweet sleep.

When Linda opened her blue eyes, the sun was so bright it shone even through the blinds. She glanced quickly at her clock.

Oh, I have slept the morning away," she moaned, "and there is so much to do! There is still a dress to buy and so many other details to take care of..."

Linda dressed quickly and ate breakfast. Then she went to the garage for her car.

That afternoon, she decided, was the most hectic on record. She tried on dresses until finally the saleslady brought one that suited her. It was a silver dinner dress with tiny straps at the shoulder. She liked it at once. The salesgirl nodded approval at the choice. Before she left the store, Linda bought shoes with ridiculous heels to go with her new dress.

By the time she returned to the apartment, she had spent almost a whole month's salary.

"This is ridiculous," she murmured to herself as she hurried from the store and back to her car. "All this trouble for one little interview."

Yet she knew she would never forget this night so, with a sigh, she went on with her appointments.

As she entered the foyer of the apartment building she walked past a mirror. The girl who looked back at her had a face that was flushed and rosy. Linda could hardly believe it was her own reflection. With a wink at the girl in the mirror, she hurried up the stairs without waiting for the elevator.

As she was eating her solitary dinner, the doorbell rang. Before she could get to the door to answer, she met Sandy – already inside!

"Hi," Sandy sang out, and walked to the kitchen.

As always, she had arrived like a windstorm. Without waiting for Linda to say anything, Sandy jumped right in.

"How come you get all the good assignments?" she complained. I would give my false eyelashes for this one!"

All the excitement of her voice was in her eyes as she continued.

"Imagine getting a chance to interview that hunk of man!" Sandy rolled her eyes and Linda could not help laughing. She was used to the way her friend exaggerated everything.

"Come on! Have dinner with me and we can talk about it," she answered. She really did want to talk because, now that the time was drawing close, she was beginning to feel very excited.

After dinner Linda showed Sandy the dress and shoes she had bought.

The only answer Sandy gave was a long, drawn out, Wow!"

"Just what does that mean" Linda demanded.

Sandy was unprepared for Linda's sudden defensive tone. It was not like her at all. Deciding not to go too far, she said smoothly, "I am just jealous because you are going instead of me."

After that, she kept to lighter subjects, but she was concerned that Linda was taking this interview much too seriously.

Linda waited for her friend to leave and then she started to get ready for her evening. She had spent most of the afternoon buying her dress and the rest of it having her hair piled high on her pretty head. She spent a good part of her time on an exquisite, delicately scented bath. Her makeup had to be perfect. Finally, it was time for the new dress, that had made Sandy raise her eyebrow curiously.

When Linda finished dressing, she stood and looked at herself in the mirror. The silver dress turned her eyes to a brilliant blue, making them sparkle like diamonds. The slippers on her tiny feet showed her long, slender legs to her advantage. Linda knew the dress looked nice on her, but she had no idea just how beautiful she really looked that evening. Her mind was busy wondering what it would be like talking to Rick Morrow.

"Will he like me?" The question came to her mind unbidden and unwanted. A blush crept into her cheeks and she reached out impatiently and snapped out the light.

II

Rick Morrow had been staring into the fireplace for several minutes, lost in some deep thought. A frown creased his brow and his face wore a tired, haggard expression. He raised his head and looked around the room. The air was filled with smoke and the shrill laughter of women. Men stood around holding wine glasses, staring vacantly and, as Rick watched, it seemed to him as though they were actors on a stage. He felt so detached from the scene – a setting he had arranged himself. Now he wondered why it seemed as though something was missing. Again, his mind strayed back to his own thoughts, his eyes staring into the roaring fireplace.

This was winter in New York - the never-ending cocktail parties, first here, then there. A wisp of memories slipped through his mind a like some forgotten ghost. Rick's frown deepened now, as he was drawn back to those days so long ago.

As always, along with the thoughts came the familiar fear running through him like ice. Would he always be so afraid of losing this success for which he had worked so hard? He ran his hand through his tousled hair and, as he did, he could feel someone watching him.

He raised his head sharply and looked right into a pair of beautiful blue eyes. They belonged to a young woman with a slender figure that would delight any man's eye. The girl was wearing a silver dress with thin straps, leaving her lovely shoulders bare. As he looked at her, Rick realized he had seen her at one of his performances just a few nights before. He had the feeling she had been watching him for some time. He crossed the room quickly and introduced himself.

"Oh yes, Mr. Morrow! I am with the Daily News. We see your picture quite often." She spoke with a friendly smile. "My name is Linda O'Connor. I was invited here for an interview, I believe."

Although she was very, very nervous standing so close to him, she tried to speak in a bantering tone. Rick took her arm and they walked across the hall to a quiet study.

Once there, he said, "All right, Miss O'Connor, let's sit in here where no one can disturb us."

He could not understand why he behaved in this manner. He had never allowed any woman in this room before! This was his sanctuary – a place where he could work or just sit and think if he preferred. As he looked at the silent little stranger standing next to him, he felt as though she somehow belonged there.

Still pursuing this thought, Rick said, "Do you like martinis? It looks as though George was expecting us."

She nodded her head, wondering who George was, as she waited for him to come back from the small bar at the end of the room. Rick pointed toward two comfortable chairs placed beside a table.

Sitting in one of the chairs, Linda accepted the drink that Rick was holding out to her. Her mind was wandering back to the time when she first arrived. She had stood in the foyer for a few minutes, watching him. His head was bowed, and she noticed a sadness on his face. Her heart had given a strange twinge, but she didn't dwell on it because that was when he looked up and caught her watching him. His mouth seemed gentle enough when he looked at her that night at the casino. Someone had hurt him deeply, she decided.

She looked around the room and knew it was a man's room. Linda approved of the deep, roomy furniture and the quiet, plain furnishings.

Rick watched her as she took inventory of his room and, for some reason, the thought that she approved pleased him. He had known many women but none of them had ever affected him the way this one did. He liked her directness and her quiet air of dignity.

They sat in a companionable silence for a while. Rick watched the firelight shine on her hair. Her presence seemed to bring a new warmth to his study.

"I understand you are one of Mr. Weston's star reporters," he offered as a beginning for her interview.

She stammered at his unexpected compliment. Rick smiled at her with that same wonderful, gentle smile she remembered. That made it much easier for her to start the questions that were part of any interview. Rick had become so familiar with the kind of woman who used any method to get what they wanted that this girl was a refreshing change for him.

Linda interviewed Rick in a general way, but she could not bring herself to ask him anything about his personal life. She was afraid to hear that there might be someone special. - someone, someplace. She finished her martini and arose from her chair.

Thank you for taking so much time with me tonight, Mr. Morrow," she said.

Rick surprised himself for the second time that night by saying, "Please call me Rick."

With a sweet smile on her lips and a lilt in her voice, Linda replied, "Thank you, Rick! And will you call me Linda?

She held out a slender hand and Rick took it in his own.

"I must go, Rick. You know, I am a working girl and morning comes all too soon."

With a wave of her hand, she stepped through the door that he held open for her.

Although the pressure of her small hand had been light, he could feel it long after she had gone. The scent of her perfume lingered in the air. Rick sat with an unlit pipe held tightly in his hand, dreading to leave the room. He knew that as soon as he did, the spell that held him would be gone.

Linda walked back to her car, all the while thinking about the last hour which had passed by so quickly.

"He is the gentlest person I have ever met," she mused and laughed softly to herself as she remembered how he had caught her looking at him. "I wonder what he was thinking that made him so sad?"

Her face wore a frown as she stepped into her car. It remained there all the way back to her apartment. Going up in the elevator, Linda looked at her hand. Strange, but she could still feel the tingle from the masculine strength of Rick's fingers. A thrill shot through her when she remembered the way he talked and his sweet attempt to make her feel at home there in his study. She reminded herself sternly that Rick had treated her as he would anyone else and that she was just being silly. She would probably never see him again. For some reason, that thought greatly troubled her.

~ ~ ~

Sandy picked her notebook up from her desk just as Linda walked into the office the next morning. It was still early, and they were the first to arrive. Linda's face usually wore a cheerful smile and she usually had a friendly joke or amusing remark to share.

Today, Sandy noticed that her friend's expression was pensive and that she seemed extremely quiet. She was sure her friend was troubled about something that concerned Rick Morrow. She was, however, determined to say nothing, though it was difficult waiting for Linda to speak first. They had always respected each other far too much to pry.

With a quiet, "Good morning, Sandy," Linda sat down and started to do a write up on last night's interview. It took her all morning, and several sheets of paper wound up in the waste basket before she was finished. Finally satisfied, Linda sat back with a sigh.

23

Mr. Weston had noticed the troubled expression on Linda's face when he arrived that morning. Saying nothing, he went on to his office. He sat at his desk and slowly turned the pages of his calendar.

"Maybe she needs a vacation," he reasoned as he watched her through the small window.

He saw her get up and start walking toward his office with the typed interview in her hand; he beckoned for her to come in even before she could lift her hand to knock.

Putting the paper on his desk, he noticed that her usually happy expression was grave and sober. She waited while he read the article. He was very pleased with it and told her so. He also added there would be a small bonus and a few days' vacation to be taken whenever she wanted them. The last was given on the spur of the moment. Mr. Weston felt a fatherly concern for Linda. She was one of his favorite people. Satisfied with his decision, he soon forgot the incident and was lost in the rush of daily chores.

Linda went back to her desk mentally rebuking herself. She made up her mind to shake off this lethargy. She had accomplished so little, she might just as well have stayed home today!

"How foolish I am, thinking of him like this," she thought. "We live in different worlds!"

A sadness crept into her heart at the thought. The futility that filled her whole being made her heart ache in anguish.

All that week she tried desperately to forget about Rick Morrow and the interview. Her face was starting to show the strain. She was not eating. A hundred times she promised herself she would not think of him again. But it did no good. She noticed that Sandy was looking at her with concern. She tried to joke and smile in an attempt to deceive Sandy, but it was several days before Sandy relaxed and seemed relieved.

Linda knew that she had satisfied everyone else, but there was no fooling herself.

III

Linda pulled her sleek little roadster into her usual parking place across the street from the office building. She sat there for a while looking out at the snow which had been falling quietly since early morning.

Aloud, she wondered, "Why must the city always be so dirty? Even the snow is mixed with the cinders and subway dirt!"

Suddenly, she found her thoughts straying back to the soft, feathery snow that fell in Maine. Some days not one track marred the beauty there.

Linda's father and mother had died in an automobile accident when she was four years old, leaving her alone except for an aunt and uncle. They had a farm in Maine but, when they became her legal guardians, the O'Connor's left their own home to come and live with her in Connecticut. It was hard for them to leave old friends and familiar surroundings, but they felt it would be much harder for Linda to adjust to a new home after her tragic loss.

Even after they moved to Connecticut, the O'Connors often took Linda to the farm for long vacations. Many times, they spent Christmas there. A soft smile touched her face as she thought about all the times her uncle had

26

taken her with him to cut a Christmas tree. The O'Connors had been just like real parents to Linda – always. She chuckled at the time Uncle Edward taught her to make a trail back to the farm house.

He had joked about it saying, "You never know when a good trail will come in handy," as they painted white streaks on many of the trees.

Linda would follow them home by herself never realizing her uncle was always just a few feet away. Although he made a game of it, she knew now that he had wanted to make sure his niece would never be lost in the deep, thick woods. It would be so easy to get lost there that, even now, Linda shuddered as she thought about it.

Thinking of the warm old farmhouse nestled at the base of the mountain brought a wave of homesickness that washed over Linda like the ocean wave. Her uncle and aunt were getting on in years now, so they didn't care to make the trip as much as they had in years before.

"But the key is always there, hanging in the shed," she murmured to herself. "Sandy could cover for me here. There really isn't that much to do." In an instant, the decision was made. "I am going to Maine this weekend!"

Spinning her car out of the spot where she had parked it just a few minutes earlier, Linda headed back for her apartment, a determined expression on her lovely face.

For the first time in days, she felt as though her world was back in focus again.

She called Mr. Weston as soon as she arrived home. He gave her the time off and said that Sandy would cover for her. Linda made a second call, this time to make a reservation on an early flight. She breathed a sigh of relief as the girl told her there was an afternoon flight leaving for Maine that very day. She laughed aloud with joy as she started pulling her heavy ski clothes from the bags hanging at the back of her closet. She had grown accustomed to heading for the sun whenever she could get away from her work. It was nice to always have a tan, but it had been quite some time since she felt this lighthearted. Before long, Linda was lost in the chore of packing.

~ ~ ~

Across the city, a moody young man sat in his study staring at nothing. The bitter lines around his mouth softened and a gentle smiled tugged at the corners. He suddenly remembered a girl who had made him change his mind about many things. Maybe there was something to look forward to after all. He shook his head impatiently.

"I must get away from here for a while," he muttered to himself, and, getting up from his chair, he started pacing across the study.

As he paced, his fingers ran through his already tousled hair.

He stopped in the middle of his pacing and thought, "Why not Bob's lodge? He's been asking me for months to come up this winter."

He and Bob had been friends for years. As soon as Bob heard his old friend's voice over the phone, he immediately invited Rick to come for a weekend of skiing.

"Just what I was about to ask you, Bob," Rick countered. "Are you sure this weekend is all right?"

Bob assured him that it would be just fine and added, "Come as soon as you can!"

Rick knew he would be able to relax and allowed to set his own pace at the lodge. No one there would demand attention unless he offered it. He was anxious to leave and, calling George into the room asked him to start packing right away.

As he made the arrangements and gave George instructions for the time he would be away, the phone rang. With a frown on his handsome face, Rick reached out to answer it. The voice on the other end made his frown deepen. It was Carol. He wondered how he could have ever found her high-pitched voice attractive. She wanted him to attend a party that night.

Trying to keep the curtness out of his voice Rick said, "I'm sorry, Carol. I have a very important engagement for tonight."

It seemed strange, even to him, but he was reluctant to tell her where he was going. Carol always had a way to showing up wherever he was. She was very angry when none of her coy pleading could sway him. Finally, she gave up.

With a sigh of relief, Rick replaced the receiver. Why, he wondered, couldn't she just leave him alone?

"Hasn't she hurt me enough already," he asked himself out loud.

She managed to irritate him even now, after all this time. He sat there thinking of their brief marriage. How could he ever have thought that he loved her? It wasn't too long after their marriage that he discovered how shallow a person Carol really was. She was so cold and vain that she hadn't even wanted children. It had hurt then, but now Rick was very glad there had been none. He would love to have kids some day but he certainly wanted a much different kind of person for their mother.

Rick chuckled dryly as he sat there by himself. It was nice to be able to do that now because there was no ache in his heart.

Bringing his thoughts back to the present, Rick went to see how far his valet had progressed with the packing. Good old George. He had all the reservations and taxi taken care of. The packing was finished, and George was now cancelling all appointments that would have to wait until the following week.

George spoke from the bedroom door. "If I may say so, sir, this vacation is just what you have been needing!" Then he added, "Shall I come along?"

Rick grinned at his valet who was also a very good friend. He knew why George wanted to come along. He would make sure Rick got plenty of rest.

"No," Rick said with a smile. "This will give you a chance to catch up on your social life.

George smiled back and without saying anything else, went back to checking the luggage.

IV

Linda stepped from the cab and hurried to the waiting plane.

"Thank God I made it," she murmured, gratefully sinking into the comfortable seat.

The voice of the stewardess filled the small cabin. "Fasten your seat belts, please," she announced importantly. The warning light flashed, its brightness emphasizing her words.

Quickly, Linda fastened her belt and leaned back with a sigh. She hadn't had time to look around as she boarded the plane and had taken the nearest available seat. She was vaguely aware that there were only about three other passengers besides herself. The trip would be a short one - less than three hours. She was glad about that. It would have been faster and easier if she had waited until the next day, and taken a jet, but she had been anxious to leave. The airfield where she would land was close to her destination and it could not accommodate a large jet anyway. Satisfied with her decision, she picked up a book that she packed in her bag. Linda did not feel like reading but at least it would help pass the boring hours ahead of her.

Although she didn't see him, Rick was just two seats behind Linda on the plane. When she boarded the plane, the person seated next to Rick had taken his attention and he did not see her come in. He could never go far before someone would recognize him. The older man seated next to him had recognized him and wanted his autograph for his grandson.

"Aren't you Rick Morrow?" he asked.

Rick smiled at the man's enthusiasm.

"Yes, I am," he replied.

Rick gave him the autograph, written on a card that his seatmate held out to him. Now, hoping to discourage any further attempts at conversation, Rick leaned back and closed his eyes. His thoughts strayed back to the night of the party. He remembered the blue-eyed girl he had met. It seemed strange to him, but he felt as though he had known her forever. She had a refreshing way of looking straight into his eyes when she spoke, yet Rick could detect a shyness when they were alone in the study.

He frowned now because, for some reason his mind had taken a turn to a subject he never allowed to stay on his mind. It was a time, not long ago, when he had collapsed while touring the country. He had only just started his career and had looked forward to fulfilling his fondest dreams. His future seemed so secure and the world was a wonderful place. He had been married for about eighteen months and Carol, his wife, was in Europe on a vacation. It hadn't taken her long to become bored with being a housewife. Rick had been left alone to face the doctor's diagnosis. He had pneumonia and would have to stay in bed for at least a month.

In the meantime, the doctors ran more tests that proved Rick to be more seriously ill than they had first suspected. When Rick left the hospital, he had to move to the country for another six months. His engagements had to be cancelled and that was the end of his tour.

Being isolated and away from the public eye for such a long time, Rick's popularity soon faded. His bitterness was complete when Carol came home and announced she was leaving him. She filed for a divorce. He wondered if it wouldn't have been so bad if she had stayed by him, but instead, she told him that she did not want to be tied to a failure.

As he sat there thinking about it, there was no sign of the usual bitterness. When had it disappeared? Strange, the feeling was only one of relief.

Shortly after Carol had left him, Rick started to get well. His friends helped him back up the ladder and, before he knew it, he was very much in demand again. He knew the parties and the engagements his friends had sent his way were the reason and for this he would always be grateful.

Rick soon realized that he was more tired than he thought. Before long, he was sound asleep. It was an uneasy sleep, filled with dreams. He was dreaming of Carol. Her greedy hands were grasping at him, wanting him back. She was always present at most of the parties he attended and, as soon as she noticed that Rick had made it back into the golden circle, she made a desperate attempt to get him to notice her again. Rick made no effort in that direction however. He had had enough of Carol and all her kind. Even in his sleep he was rejecting her.

Suddenly an urgent voice broke into his dreams. It took him a while to become fully awake. The words were clear now. He could hear the stewardess saying, "Fasten your seat belts." Her voice carried a strained quality.

At first, he thought they were about to land. But then Rick noticed how quiet everything was and he felt the fear that grasped the passengers. Realizing for the first time that they were in danger, Rick quickly reached for his seat belt, but it was too late. The small plane, buffeted by strong winds, suddenly struck against something solid. That was all Rick remembered before the blackness descended.

~ ~ ~

Linda had put her book aside and was dozing when the stewardess made her frantic appeal. She became fully awake and, looking out of the little window beside her, noticed the snow swirling by at a tremendous speed. She was well aware that something was wrong. She guessed that the plan was overshooting the runway. Strange how detached she felt - as though it were happening to someone else. Just then, a large white cloud came swirling at her.

V

Linda's eyes opened slowly. She didn't realize where she was at first.

"Oh, I feel so cold," she murmured. Then she remembered the snow swirling outside the plane. She lifted her arm to brush the hair from her eyes. As she did, a sharp pain sliced through it. Looking down she could see that her coat sleeve was ripped away and blood was slowly drying on her sweater. Linda felt a scream rising to her lips. She fought the panic with all the willpower she had. Still too dazed to grasp the full situation, she wondered, "Where am I? What happened?"

As she sat in the darkness, her mind started to clear. The plane had crashed.

"But this isn't the runway..." she thought.

It was all flashing before her now like some horrible nightmare. She moved quickly to her feet but, with a gasp, she sank back into the snow. Her ankle had been sprained too. Linda felt the scream rising to her lips again.

"I will not be afraid," she said aloud.

Hearing her own voice in the awful stillness steadied her as nothing else could have.

Looking slowly around, the frightened girl could make out the burned-out remains of the plane. She could see no one else around. Linda realized that she had to do something so, slowly, she examined her arms and legs to see just how badly she had been hurt. When she was sure that her injuries consisted of one cut arm and a sprained ankle, Linda breathed a relieved sight. At least she would be able to drag herself away from this place.

She decided that any activity would be better than just sitting. A person could freeze to death doing that, as she well knew. Strange that her Uncle Ed's face should run through her mind right at this moment. How she wished he was with her.

It wasn't snowing now, but Linda was so cold she knew that she must have been lying there for some time. After several unsuccessful tries, the injured girl was able to get to her feet and hobble around. The numbness helped to keep her from feeling the pain.

Linda felt very much alone as she moved slowly toward the darkness of the cliff. The moon was peeking out from behind the clouds and the remains of the plane stood like some hulking giant.

"It's a miracle that I am here at all" she whispered into the lonely night.

There wasn't one piece of the interior of the plane left. Linda could find nothing except the twisted metal sitting there beneath the shadows of the over-hanging cliff. A huge shudder ran through her and the sad-faced girl sat down, weary and defeated.

Taking off the remains of her coat, she clenched her teeth and slowly worked the sweater over her head. Using pieces of her tattered blouse, Linda managed to fashion a bandage for her arm and then one for her ankle. Her arm was throbbing, and her fingers were very numb. But, after a while, she managed to do a fair job. Even this small accomplishment gave Linda a feeling of security. Now she started to feel more hopeful. Maybe she could get out of here. Glancing around, she noticed that the plane had landed in a small ravine. Something about the place nagged at her tired and dazed mind. She had the feeling that she had been there before.

"I must be getting delirious," she sighed. Then panic struck at her again. "I am out of sight here. No one will ever see me!"

Feeling completely beaten, Linda was almost ready to give up when she heard something. She listened for a moment and decided it was just the wind moaning in the trees.

"No! There it is again."

Her heart started to beat faster at the thought that she might not be the only survivor after all. The sound she heard was a moan; Linda was certain of that. It seemed to be coming from a small patch of brush just a few feet from where she found herself after the crash. Moving as fast as her injured leg would allow, it took some time cover the distance. Now she could make out a dark figure and she knew instinctively that it was a man.

"I must help," she whispered, kneeling carefully in the snow beside him. He looked so white and still that Linda was not sure he was even alive. But, just then, he moaned again.

As she recognized the man lying there, she cried out, "Rick! Rick," she called out. "Rick, speak to me! Please! Say something!"

Looking at the face that had become so familiar to her these past few days, she could not stop the stream of tears. She pulled him over to her and, with his head resting on her lap, Linda cried until she could cry no more.

Even as she continued to cry, the heartbroken girl was gently examining his face. She had noticed the blood caked on his head and face. It had come from a bad cut on the side of his temple. There didn't seem to be any other injuries. Linda pulled the remainder of her blouse from her coat pocket. She had stuffed it there when she put her sweater and coat back on. All the time she was making a bandage and crudely wrapping it around his head she kept wondering why he had been on that plane with her. Strange, she thought to herself, that she hadn't seen him.

As Linda sat there, holding Rick, a voice in her heart kept saying over and over, "Please, God, don't let him die." For now, she could only hold him, and try to keep him warm.

"I must do something," she thought.

Although she felt certain that no one could have survived besides the two of them, once more she decided to take a look. Convinced, Linda started to go back to where Rick lay. Looking up at the tree she was leaning against, fighting for strength to go one, she noticed a white streak of paint. Her heart gave a giant leap!

"Oh, yes!" she cried out.

God had heard her prayer after all. This paint could only mean one thing. They had crashed close to the farmhouse.

"That's why the ravine looked so familiar," she marveled. But suddenly as her joy had come, it was gone. "How am I going to get him down there alone?"

The thought of the big house and food urged her tired mind to think. Although the ground was buried deep in snow, the cold night air had made it hard and easy to walk on.

"If only I could make Rick understand."

She managed to get Rick to his feet. He was only half conscious and the going was very slow. His weight on her arm was almost more than Linda could bear, but she wouldn't let him go. She knew now that he was more important to her than life itself!

She struggled along, checking each tree for a marker. Each time Rick would slide to the ground, Linda would tug until he was on his feet once more. Rick's moans kept her mind alert. She was so worried about him that she could almost forget her own pain.

As they slid and crawled down the snow-covered mountain Rick fell from her arms. Exhausted, she sat beside him.

"I cannot go on," Linda said aloud.

Her arms were so numb with the cold and the house, she was certain, was far away. Pushing herself, Linda managed to get up once again. As she struggled with Rick he seemed to understand how important it was for him to get up too.

The first streaks of dawn were just coming over the horizon when, right ahead, Linda could make out the shape of the farmhouse. She could hardly believe her eyes. They had made it!

Linda gently leaned Rick against the shed and ran inside. Even her sprained ankle was forgotten for the moment. The key was hanging right where she knew it would be. Before long, the two, tired people were inside and away from the raw, bitter, northern cold.

Because she was so cold, the first thing Linda did was start a blazing fire in the old fireplace. By the time she accomplished this, Rick had lapsed into unconsciousness again.

She thanked heaven she been sensible enough to get him to the sofa as they entered the room. Going to the bedroom just off the hall, Linda scooped up all the blankets on the iron bed stand. She covered Rick as he was, clothes and all. Then, she put several large logs on the fire and curled up on the floor, wrapped snugly in her blanket. Soon she was fast asleep.

She had not even noticed that the big snowflakes were falling again. It would be much later before she realized how lucky they were that the farm had been so close to the mountain where the plane had crashed.

VI

Linda was having such a beautiful dream. She could feel strong arms holding her in a firm embrace. With a sigh, she snuggled closer. She must have drifted off into a sounder sleep for a short while. When she finally awoke, she could feel Rick's muscular body so close to hers that she sat up, startled.

Gently, Rick pulled her back down near him again. Little brown imps of mischief danced in fun, deep in his green eyes. Linda's own eyes darkened in surprise but before she could move or speak, he bent until his lips were on her own. His kiss was so filled with hunger and, although Linda knew she should stop him, her own lips betrayed her, clinging to his. She had no desire to resist or object. The love she had felt before came rushing through her again. Linda knew that she was in love with this strange young man and, without hesitation, she returned his kiss with all the love in her heart.

Rick moved his head and looked at her.

"I don't know where we are, or how we got here, but I do know one thing. I love you! I've been watching you sleep and I just couldn't wait for you to wake up so that I could tell you. Do you hear me? I love you!"

Linda smiled for the first time in a good many hours. Rick certainly looked as though he was going to be fine.

"Yes, Rick. I hear you," she whispered.

As she spoke the words, her fingers stroked his cheek. She touched the deep dimple at the corner of his mouth. She had noticed it first of all. For some reason, it made his smile gentler than any she had ever seen before. She noticed the deep cleft in his chin and his strong wide jaw. How she did love him.

He bent his head and kissed her again. She did not draw away. There was no coyness about her – just a mature sweetness that had attracted Rick right away, the first time he had seen her.

Rick felt that there could be no other love for him again. He held her gently and vowed to himself that he would protect her from all harm. This was a love that would endure for all of their lives.

Linda hated to leave the warmth of his arms, but the long afternoon shadows made her realize that they had slept most of the day.

Slowly she arose from the warm blanket and said, "I'll go and see what I can find for us to eat."

Rick helped her take a few steps and, when he saw that she could make it without help, he went to put more logs on the fire. As he looked outside, he noticed that the snow was piled high and he knew it would be some time before anyone could get to the them. He did not say anything to Linda because he did not want to alarm her. She had been through enough already. Rick knew how difficult it must have been for her, trying to get him through the snow and into the farmhouse. He could hardly recall any of the trip. He could only remember hearing Linda's pleading voice, begging him to keep trying, each time he had stumbled and fallen into the snow.

Once the fire was replenished, there was nothing else for Rick to do so he went to see what he could do to help Linda. She found cans of soup and boxes of crackers. There was meat and bacon in the freezer. Linda knew there would be canned fruit and vegetables in the cellar, for later meals. Her aunt still canned and women from the valley always put something in the cellar for the hunters who might be stranded there.

Linda's family had made many friends over the years they lived there, and the farmers made sure that the O'Connor farm was never without fuel or food.

Rick made the coffee. Then each of them carried a steaming tray into the living room by the warm fire. It was difficult for the slender girl, but she managed to limp back by herself. They sat down on the floor with the trays before them. Rick reached over and touched her hair. His fingers moved down gently until they reached her lips. Without a word, Linda's lips kissed the hand that had caressed her face just a moment before. The lovers sat quietly for some time, only speaking once in a while about their ordeal and how lucky they were to be alive. Linda snuggled her head against Rick's rough shirt and closed her eyes. She was so very happy.

Suddenly, Rick placed a hand on either side of her face.

"You saved my life today. And now it belongs to you," he teased. Then he added, "You do know what that means, don't you?"

Linda looked into his laughing eyes and she wrinkled her nose at him.

Looking right at him, she asked, "No. What does it mean, Rick?"

His teasing glance changed to one of complete seriousness.

"It means I want you to marry me, funny face," he replied. Linda's breath caught someplace in her throat. She hadn't expected this. It was so wonderful, she felt as though she must be dreaming.

Rick's arms had tightened around her, and his lips were against her hair. All she could say was, "I love you, Rick. And I guess I have right from the start. I want to be your wife more than anything else in the world."

As she finished speaking she could feel tears burning at her eyelids. Linda was thinking about how close to death they had both come just yesterday and now, today, her world was new and beautiful. The thought of being married to Rick was on that overwhelmed her. She knew there was no one in the world that she would change places with, even if she could.

~ ~ ~

Night had come, silently stealing into the big room where Rick and Linda were sitting. The fireplace was throwing shadows over the room. Linda remembered the oil lamps in the kitchen where her aunt always kept them. She went out and picked them up from the shelf. Bringing them back to the living room, she placed them on small tables. Rick lit them both and they cast a cheerful glow about the room.

Rick moved quietly but efficiently making a fire so that it would last throughout the night. Linda made beds for them right in front of the fireplace. They decided that this would be warmer than trying to sleep in the un-heated bedrooms. There were pajamas left by Uncle Edward for Rick to wear and Linda found a pair of her own. Soon they were ready to crawl into their makeshift beds and go to sleep.

Linda fell asleep at once. She was much more tired than she wanted Rick to know. The pain in her arm was gone and it looked like it was healing, but the ankle still was giving her some trouble. She had been so happy to see how much better Rick was when he awakened that she hadn't wanted to worry him about her small sprain. Sometime in the night, Linda felt Rick's arms pull her close to him. She soon felt warm and went right back to sleep. She was at peace with the world and her sleep was deep and dreamless.

Rick had spent a restless night. He was worried about getting Linda safely back to civilization. The farm had been their salvation when they needed it, but it could be their grave if he could not find a way out. He wondered how long it would be before anyone passed this way. No one would know where the plane had crashed. Its charred remains were probably covered with snow by now. He noticed Linda murmuring in her sleep and knew she was cold. He reached over and pulled her close to him. Looking down into her sleeping face, a great wave of love washed over him. He had known her for such a short time and yet, he couldn't remember any time when he had not loved her. Rick held her close for the rest of the night. He didn't even realize how drowsy he had become until, suddenly, he too was fast asleep.

Linda awoke to the sound of Rick in the kitchen making breakfast. She was just ready to get up and join him when he came into the room with a tray of food. He had found syrup in the cellar and had made some hotcakes. He called her name as he came into the room.

"Okay sleepy head! It's time for breakfast!" He put the tray down and ruffled her tousled hair.

Today, they both felt much better and it was easier to talk about the crash. Linda told him what she had been doing on the plane and how she had planned to rent a sleigh and come out to the farm. Then she asked Rick where he had been headed. When he mentioned the name of Bob's lodge, Linda told him that it was not far from the village. As she thought about Rick's other world, a fear stole into her heart and it was evident on her face. Her thoughts raced on.

"Maybe I cannot fit into Rick's world," she told herself.

She looked so sad, Rick demanded, "Come back to me, darling," as he walked around the tray to stand at her side.

Something had frightened her, he was sure. He put his arms around her and, with a sigh, Linda rested her head close to him. Rick kissed her and, with his arm still around her, walked her to the sofa facing the winter world outside. Linda's troubled thoughts just seemed to melt away.

Rick looked into her face, tilted up at him, and said, "Dearest Love, life would mean nothing without you. Always remember that."
It was almost as though he had read her thoughts.

They talked about getting married in the summer.

"Let's make it as soon as possible." Rick said. "Now that I have found you, I want you to be with me always."
Linda was so happy at the prospect of being Mrs. Rick Morrow, she nodded her head in agreement. They finally decided on an early June. wedding. It wasn't too far in the future and it would allow plenty of time for all the arrangements to be made.

Later, Rick found some playing cards that had been left in a desk drawer by Linda's uncle, and they played cards for a while.

Although Linda had no fear and was quite relaxed, Rick was concerned about her ankle and the possibility that it might be some time before anyone found them.

VII

It seemed to the O'Connors as though they had been waiting forever for some news about their niece. Linda had been missing for two days now and there had been no sign of the missing aircraft or the people in it. The two older people prayed as they sat waiting for some word.

"She is all the family we have, Ed," Aunt Susan sobbed.

Trying to soothe his wife, he answered, "She will be found soon, Mother. Don't worry. Linda is a very sensible girl."

After he finished speaking, the gray-haired Mr. O'Connor sat in thoughtful silence for a few minutes. Then, he spoke again. "Susan, we are going to Maine!"

His voice was an explosion that filled the silence.

"I can drive there in less than three hours, Mother. And we know those mountains better than anyone else."

His wife knew that it was true and that, if Linda was to be found, he was the man who would do it.

Aunt Susan was already on the stairs as she called back over she shoulder, "I will pack while you get the car out."

Uncle Ed knew better than to argue with his wife. Her mind was made up. He just nodded and headed for the closet where his coat was hanging. By the time he had the car ready, the old suitcase, that they used so seldom now, was sitting in the hall. There was a supply of jackets and flashlights also ready for use once they arrived. By the time Uncle Ed had the car packed and filled with all the things Aunt Susan thought they might need, it was four o'clock in the morning.

The man behind the wheel was an excellent driver, and it was a good thing. The snow was piled high on both sides of the road. He guided the big car onto the highway with ease and they both gave a sigh, glad to be on their way at last.

It was slow driving because the highway was slick from the new layer of snow that had fallen the day before.

It was daylight when they finally saw the sleepy little village ahead. Uncle Ed drove to the only gas station in the area and parked his car in the lot where he had parked so many times before. Aunt Susan sat in the car and waited while he went to the nearby stable and rented a sleigh with a patient old horse to carry them out to the farm. It would be impossible for them to get there any other way, as the snow lay high and untouched all around the tiny village. Soon the sleigh was piled high with luggage and food. With a final tuck of the lap robe around his wife, the O'Connors were on their way.

For some reason that even he could not explain, Uncle Edward was very anxious to get to the farm. They loved the old house, tucked away, so far out in the country. Although neither of them ever said so, they missed the quiet peacefulness of their home. The familiar surroundings brought tears flooding into Aunt Susan's tired old eyes. The snow capped the beautiful peaks of the distant mountain tops. The fields lay white and untouched all around them. They passed an occasional farmhouse where smoke was already starting to curl from the chimneys.

Silently, Uncle Edward was deciding what he would do once they arrived. He would get the snowshoes out and start up the mountain as soon as he had breakfast. He knew Aunt Susan would be as anxious as he was, and that she would not give him any argument. If Linda was in those mountains, he would find her. But even as he thought about it, he knew that it would take a miracle to keep anyone alive this long.

The weather was bitter cold this morning. He remembered how Linda had filled their lives, taking the place of the children they could never have. They always spoke of her as their child – never anything else.

She, in return, had considered them her parents. No one could have asked for a more loving daughter. She never forgot their anniversary or a birthday. Even when she moved to the city, she had insisted that they visit her often. The weary man tried to think of something else as he felt his eyes misting. Suppose she was hurt. At the thought, he gave himself a mental shake-down. Aunt Susan must not even guess that such a thought had crossed his mind.

Soon the sleigh turned onto the familiar old land that ran back to the house. As they got closer they could see smoke coming from the chimney. Aunt Susan reached out and touched her husband's arm.

"Who could it be, Ed," she asked anxiously.

Shaking his head in bewilderment, his hand gave a tug at the reins. The horse started to move faster. When they arrived, Uncle Ed jumped from the sleigh, almost before the horse stopped moving. He quickly threw the reins over the porch rail and moved around the other side to help his wife climb down. As they stepped through the hall door they caught the unmistakable aroma of coffee. It smelled good to the hungry travelers.

With a quick glance at the blankets, rumpled and empty on the floor of the living room, the disturbed furniture and the blazing fire in the fireplace, Mrs. O'Connor stepped closer to her husband.

Together, they walked toward the kitchen wondering who they would find there. They gasped in unison at the strange young man standing by the stove calmly making breakfast. He was wearing a pair of uncle Edward's pajamas and an old pair of house slippers that looked very familiar as well.

"Who are you, young man?"

The man who stood in the kitchen was too stunned to ask anything more. Aunt Susan noticed his bandaged head and his pale face.

"My name is Rick Morrow. Is this your home?"

By now, Aunt Susan, could stand it no longer. She walked over to the stranger and asked, "How did you hurt your head?"

Rick started to explain about the plane crash but before he could say more than two words, Aunt Susan interrupted him.

"Please excuse me for being rude. But please tell us if there were any other survivors. You see, our niece was on that plane."

Tears were running down her wrinkled cheeks.

Immediately, Rick realized who they were.

"Oh! How stupid of me. Of course! You are Linda's family!"

He told them that she was asleep in the bedroom and safe as could be. This brought such a look of relief to the faces of the O'Connors that it was a pleasure for Rick to see. He was glad he had carried Linda into the bedroom and had insisted that she stay in the big iron bed while he made the living room warmer and started to make breakfast.

Aunt Susan had to see for herself that her niece was safe. She tiptoed into the bedroom and saw Linda fast asleep. The bed had proven to be so comfortable that Linda just had to relax. She had fallen into a deep sleep before she knew what happened.

Satisfied that all was well with Linda, Aunt Susan carefully closed the door and went back to the kitchen. Her happy face told Uncle Ed all he needed to know.

The three strangers introduced themselves again and then they all sat down to eat Rick's delicious breakfast. Aunt Susan insisted that both men should let her take over the chore of serving the food. It made her happy to be able to work around the big farm kitchen again.

Rick told the couple how Linda had saved his life, and, in return, they thanked him over and over again for taking such good care of her. Their beaming faces were a delight to see.

They asked so many questions that Rick could hardly keep up with them. He did his best to tell them all that had happened. Mr. O'Connor decided that he would ride back into town as soon as possible and alert the authorities so that they would be able to find the plane and identify the people who had perished in the crash.

After several cups of good coffee, the O'Connors and Rick were getting along well. Just as they were about to leave the table, the kitchen door swung open. A tousled head came into view and, with a cry of delight, Linda recognized her aunt and uncle. The reunion was one of tears mixed with laughter. Again, they sat down and, while Linda ate, they heard again what had occurred before their arrival.

Suddenly, Aunt Susan noticed her niece – almost as though it were for the first time. Something was different about her. Her happiness was more than just the excitement of being found. He aunt was sure of that. As she watched, she noticed the look on Linda's face whenever she looked at Rick. Her aunt recognized the tender expression of love and quietly nodded to herself as Rick returned the love with a smile filled with quiet happiness.

Later, Linda and her aunt went into the living room to talk and clean up. Uncle Edward and Rick stayed behind, lingering over their coffee, discussing events that had taken place.

The older man pulled a pipe from his pocket and started to fill it thoughtfully. He was still wondering about the look that had passed between this young man and his niece. Holding the unlighted pipe in his hand, uncle Edward tried to think of a way to bring the subject into the conversation. Looking for just the right words, he finally spoke.

"Rick, Linda is the only child that we will ever have, and I want you to know how grateful we are to you."

It was the only thing he could think of to say and, under his bushy brows, his brown eyes wore a troubled expression.

Rick had noticed the unspoken question in the other man's voice. He decided to tell Mr. O'Connor about the plans he and Linda had already made. Now, he answered the question by saying,

"Your niece is the most precious thing that has ever happened to me. I love her more than anything else in this world. I have asked Linda to marry me and I hope that you will give us your blessing.

The older man sat for some time without saying anything. Then he arose and walked around the table. He put his hand on Rick's shoulder. He had liked the boy the minute he saw him standing there in the ill-fitting pajamas.

It was so like Linda to wait this long, then fall in love almost overnight.

Linda told Aunt Susan the news as they worked in the bedroom, picking up blankets and talking about the things that had happened. Her aunt was delighted. Like her husband, she liked Rick right away. With their arms happily linked together, the two women walked out to the kitchen to talk about the sudden turn of events. The men had just finished talking.

Aunt Susan went over to Rick and kissed him. Rick and Linda stood side by side, and their happiness was a thing of beauty to the couple who watched.

Rick accompanied Mr. O'Connor to the village right after lunch. He wanted to call his agent in New York. Uncle

Edward would call the authorities and then, he and Rick would ride back to the farm in the rented sleigh.

Rick made all his calls and, when both of the men were finished, they walked to the nearby store for food and other items they would need for the few days that would follow.

It was late before they started back to the farm. As they turned into the lane, the lights of the farmhouse were a welcome sight. Rick knew he would never forget the days he had spent her with Linda. They were wonderful days that he would always treasure. The men walked into the house and smelled the delicious aromas that only come from home baked foods.

After dinner, everyone sat around the fire in the living room. Rick talked about his agent and how excited he had been to hear Rick's voice. Rick had also called his apartment and talked to George. George was not alone however. Carol was there and, when she knew Rick was alive, she insisted on talking to him. Rick decided not to mention this to Linda or her family.

Now he sat with a frown on his handsome face, remembering the conversation. Carol wanted to fly right out there to be with him. He had exploded.

"No, Carol! I do not want you to come out here! I will be back in New York in a few days. We can talk then."

The frown was still on his face as he looked up and saw Linda watching him. Her own face was unhappy with her concern for him.

She got up from her chair and walked into the big kitchen beyond. There she stood, looking out the window as the darkness stretched as far as the white snow would allow.

She didn't turn around as Rick came into the room, but she could feel his presence there. He walked up behind her and put his arm around her waist. She leaned against him with a contented sight. It was so beautiful there. How she wished they never had to leave.

As they stood in the silence, the old hall door creaked open. Linda heard the booming voice of the doctor as he spoke to her uncle. She didn't know that her uncle and Rick had stopped to see the doctor that afternoon. Aunt Susan had already placed cups and saucers on the table for them. With a quick kiss on the back of her graceful neck, Rick turned Linda around and they walked back to the table to greet the new-comer.

Dr. Nelson had brought her into the world. He was one of Linda's favorite people. She leaned over and kissed the weathered face. He patted her cheek.

Then, giving her a stern look, he said, "All right now young lady! Let's see just how much damage has been done to that ankle."

His slow, New England drawl always delighted Linda.

She grinned at him and retorted, "Yes, Sir!"

After a careful examination, the doctor told her he was sure she would live to be very old. She chuckled. This was exactly what he told her ever since she was a child.

He put a fresh bandage on her arm, but her ankle was so much better, it did not require one. Dr. Nelson had taken care of Rick earlier in the day and now he said in his best, no-nonsense voice, "I do not want either one of my patients to leave her for at least another two days."

Turning to Aunt Susan he said, "I am depending on you to see that they follow my instructions, Sue."

Once she assured him that no one would leave for at least that length of time, they turned to their coffee.

After the doctor left, the O'Connors and Rick sat in the large living room reading the papers that the men had brought back from the village. Linda returned to reading a book she had started some time earlier. She was so happy that her family liked Rick so very much.

"But then, how could they help it? He's such a wonderful person!"

Her mind ran on. As she sat, lost in happy thoughts, her aunt walked over to her, kissed her and, patting her on the cheek, went into the little bedroom, closing the door softly behind her. Uncle Ed said goodnight a short time later and he too went into the little room off the living room. The young couple were left alone, and Rick moved over to sit beside Linda on the old sofa that had held so many lovers before them.

The firelight danced on her hair and Rick could not resist the urge to touch a heavy strand that fell over her shoulder. His light touch made Linda look up at him. She marveled at the thought that there was something new to love about her Rick each time she looked at him. Her heart raced at the thought that all his love was reserved just for her now. Her fingers traced the outline of his lips and rested in the dimpled hollow at the corner of his mouth. He held her hand and kissed each finger before he let it go. She was blushing, but her glance was steady as they looked into each other's eyes. His glance made her feel as though he was kissing her – several seconds before he finally did.

VIII

The next day, people started to arrive. The first person to arrive was Rick's agent. He made the trip by helicopter. As soon as he saw that Rick was able to travel, he wanted Rick to accompany him and leave at once.

Aunt Susan stepped in at this point and showed a stubborn streak that Linda had never seen before.

"Rick is staying for at least two more days," she announced. Her small chin was set in determination. "That is doctor's orders, young man!"

Rick stood by grinning while his agent stammered and stuttered. In the agent's world, he gave the orders and people jumped. But he soon saw that this would never do here in the country. It was finally decided that the agent would stay with them until Rick could leave.

Linda was certain that her aunt felt like throwing him out in the snow, and her happiness grew just knowing how much her aunt had already grown to like Rick. But her heart felt heavy when her family urged her to ride back to Connecticut with them for a day of rest before returning to New York. She could not refuse them. The decision was made; when Rick and his agent left, she would accompany her aunt and uncle to Connecticut.

The agent spent the two days making sketches of the farmhouse. He accompanied the press and other authorities to make sketches of the crash. He intended to use their misfortune to full advantage and, although Rick was hesitant, he realized it would be a boon to his popularity. It would also be wise to have a big welcome home party for Rick, the agent decided.

While he was busy planning all this, Linda stood looking outside and noticed that it was quite dark now. She glanced over at Rick, and with a sparkle in her eyes that dared him, she headed for the hall. They grabbed jackets and boots, slipped them on and went outside while the agent sat talking. He never noticed that he was quite alone.

The moon shone white and round overhead and the stars seemed to glitter and dance in the evening sky. In the distance, the mountains stood white and cold in their majestic splendor. The pine trees cast shadows as the wind murmured through their branches. The magic of the beautiful night was in the young lovers as they walked through the snow, hand in hand. Suddenly, Linda dashed

73

away from Rick and, with a soft laugh, made a snowball and threw it at him.

"You little devil! I'll fix you for that," Rick called after her, chasing her awkwardly as he tried to run through the thick white mounds.

In a few minutes the snowballs were flying back and forth. Finally, laughing and out of breath, Rick caught up with her and dragged her down into the feathery snow. He rubbed her face with the white stuff and teased her tenderly. He looked at her now, her cheeks pink from the cold snow and her eyelashes sparkling with the drops of water as the snow melted against her warm skin. Rick dropped beside her and pulling her close to him, he kissed her – gently at first and then with an urgency that made her breathless.

When he did take his lips away from hers he said, "Why did we take so long to meet?"

Linda covered his lips with her hand.

"Please, dearest, let's not ever look back. Let's pretend that we have known each other forever because that's how I feel. Today is the important time. We love each other now and that's all that really counts. Isn't it?"

Rick agreed. I never stopped thinking about you after that night in my study, darling. When you left, the rooms were empty and lonely. I guess that's why I wanted to get away from New York."

He had been speaking slowly and suddenly he knew why he had been so restless.

"I am only happy when we are together. Always remember that, Linda." He was so serious when he spoke.

Linda watched his face. He looked down now and his expression became gentle again.

"I love you, funny face" he said as he kissed her again.

They started walking slowly, stopping to look at each other and to kiss again. Their love was so new and so beautiful that they didn't want to share it with anyone yet.

75

The night was starting to turn bitter and Rick said, "Come on, darling! I can't have you catching pneumonia."

She knew that Rick would be leaving her soon and she clung to his hand as they walked back toward the beckoning light of the house.

~ ~ ~

When Aunt Susan looked at her niece the next morning, she knew the radiant look in her eyes was not from the cold winter air. Her heart sang for this girl she loved so dearly. For so long she had hoped that a nice man would come along and make Linda realize how wonderful love could be. Although she and her husband both wanted to know Rick much better, there could be no doubt how much Linda loved him. She knew they could never repay him for the wonderful care he had given Linda.

Neighbors and other well-wishers had been coming all afternoon and now the family was weary. The snow plows had been busy cleaning the long country road and Uncle Edward would be able to bring the car out for the long trip home.

The authorities had been into the mountainous section to check the remains of the plane. They had found just what Rick and Linda had described to them. After the last person had gone down the road, everyone breathed a sigh of relief.

It was nice to be the center of attention," Linda thought to herself, "but it did get tiring."

She felt detached from all the hectic activity that had surrounded them all day. The family decided to go to bed early because the next day promised to be just as hectic as this one had been.

The old house stood bathed in the bright moonlight and the stars shone down on the sprawling old buildings that had been a haven to Rick and Linda when they needed one so desperately.

When Linda awoke, the first thing she thought of was Rick.

"Today Rick will leave me and go back to New York."

She watched the first gray of dawn creep over her room and, with a sigh, she crept quietly out of bed. She slipped into her ski suit and boots and, moving through the shadows like a small ghost, she made her way outside.

The brisk morning air brought a gasp from her lips as she walked down the lane. Her ankle was almost completely healed now; she walked with hardly any limp at all. At the end of the lane she came to an old pine bench. Her uncle had built the bench many years ago when she was just a tiny child. Linda brushed the snow away and sat down. This was a special place and she had come here often to think about her problems, or simply to dream.

Now the young girl sat quietly and looked pensively into the distance. She knew her love had to leave, and she must be smiling when he went. She would see him in a few days; then, everything would be all right again. Her love was so new that she was afraid it would disappear.

Looking up at the blue sky, she prayed, "Please God, take care of him. I love him so much."

The lonely little figure, dressed in the white ski suit, blended into the background and, until she moved, no one would notice her. She sat quietly for a long time. She hadn't realized so much time had passed until the door opened, and she saw Rick striding down the land. He didn't notice her, so she stood up and called to him.

As he came toward her she saw that he was wearing a grim expression. He took both her hands in one of his and shaking his head at her he said, "Please, don't ever do that again. I thought we had lost you."

The look in his eyes made her want to cry. She threw her arms around his neck and kissed him. As she drew back she told him something he would always remember.

"Rick," she started, "I was sitting her thinking how much I love you and that I never want to be separated from you again – not even for one day. Now you have shown me that your love is the same as mine. Oh, Rick, always love me this way."

She had whispered the last so low he could hardly hear what she was saying. As they stood here, holding each other in a close embrace, there was no need for further words.

Rick suddenly remembered that Aunt Susan had sent him looking for Linda and now they hurried, hands clinging tightly together, back up the lane to the house.

They said very little over breakfast and Rick lingered over his coffee as long as he could. His agent was impatient to get started but he did not want to upset Aunt Susan again. The older people walked outside to the waiting helicopter and gave the two lovers a few precious moments alone.

"It won't be long, darling, Rick said, "Just tomorrow and then we will be together again."

 When he finished speaking, Linda could only look at him with all her love shining in her eyes. He turned toward her as she stood in the doorway and slowly waved. As the helicopter door closed, he was swallowed up and the big craft rose into the air. In an instant, he was lost from sight. Linda ran upstairs to her room and, throwing herself across the bed, cried for the first time since she had arrived at the farmhouse. She sobbed until she was completely exhausted and then fell into a deep, dreamless sleep.

Her aunt looked in on her and, nodding her head, went back downstairs to start getting the farm ready before they would leave it again – maybe for the last time. The tired woman knew that she could never come to live here again and the thought of it made her sad. Her young years had been spent here with her Edward. They had been very much like Linda and her young man then.

Pushing the thoughts from her mind, she started folding sheets and bedding to be packed away again.

When Linda woke, her aunt tried very hard to keep her busy. She had Linda run to the basement for boxes and then to the pantry for other things – anything to keep her young mind off Rick. Soon they would be on their way to Connecticut and everything would be all right again.

It seemed an eternity to Linda before the last blanket was folded and the final latch was secured on the farmhouse. What had seemed so beautiful and warm was just a snowbound farm now, way out in the country. She had only one thought. She wanted to be with Rick.

Uncle Ed finished taking the last pieces of luggage outside and was packing them in the trunk. Finally, the motor started, and they were on their way. Once on the highway, the car moved smoothly, and Linda started to feel sleepy once more. Before she knew it, her aunt was shaking her.

"Wake up, dear. We are home."

Linda could hardly believe they had made the trip that quickly. Getting unsteadily out of the car, she helped Uncle Ed as he carried the bags inside.

The house felt so warm and cozy and Linda could feel the tiredness running out of her body. Aunt Susan led the way, turning lights on as she went.

Linda felt a sense of security every time she stood in the spacious hall of her home. She had lived here all her life except for the visits to the farm. She kissed her aunt and uncle and went directly upstairs to her own bedroom. Opening the bedroom door, Linda stopped to look at the room through the eyes of a woman. This room had remained like a sanctuary after she left home. It was always crisp and clean. The yellow organdy curtains had wide ruffles and they matched the bedspread on the huge cherry four-poster bed. The bed had belonged to her parents and Linda was very proud of it. Her rug was emerald green splashed with huge yellow roses. She loved the yellow roses so much. Her uncle had grown one and had called it the Linda Rose. He loved to tease her about it and she was sure he would mention it before she left this time.

A silver vase sat on the mantle over the white marble fireplace and she looked at it now. Though it stood empty, she knew that when summer arrived it would always have a yellow bud in it.

Picking up her robe, she headed for a warm bath. When she came out of the bathroom, she put on a fleecy yellow gown and slid into her bed with a sigh. She was smiling when she fell asleep. The smile stayed there for a long time.

Linda awoke to the ringing of the telephone. It took her a minute to remember where she was. Her aunt called to her and she jumped out of bed and headed for the hall, pulling her robe on as she went. When she picked up the extension, Linda heard Rick's voice.

"Hello, darling! I missed you so much that I couldn't wait to see you, so I decided to call."

"Hello Rick, "Linda answered breathlessly. He had taken her by surprise. "It's so good to hear your voice."

"I love you," she added, suddenly feeling the need to express her love for him.

They talked for a while. Rick told her that the party that was to be given in his honor would be held on the following night. He wanted Linda to catch an early morning flight, so he could meet her.

After Rick said goodbye, she stood looking at the phone, still hearing the sound of his voice. There was much to be done and Linda shook off her thoughts of Rick for the moment, hurrying back to her room to get dressed.

The day flew by with neighbors coming in to hear about Linda's harrowing experience and to wish her well. She was sorry that she would have to leave her aunt and uncle so soon, but they seemed cheerful and grateful for her safe return. Knowing she could never repay them for the love and care they had lavished on her, she tried to be patient and spend as much time as possible helping her aunt and talking to the man who had been a real father to her.

~ ~ ~

"It isn't easy for people in love to be patient," Linda decided as she waited for the familiar airport to appear below. When she stepped off the plan, Rick was right there, waiting, as he had promised. Her kissed her soundly and the people around them smiled as they went on their way. It was as though they had been separated for two years rather than two days. However, Linda didn't mind the intensity of his kiss. In fact, she liked it very much.

Rick's big car was waiting, and he put Linda carefully in before he went around to the other side. Linda loved to watch him drive. His firm grip on the wheel, and his wonderful self-assurance, always gave her a feeling of security. She noticed now, as they drove across the city, that they were not headed for her apartment, but for Rick's. She looked her question at him and, smiling, Rick said, "George would not have it any other way. He insisted we should let him make breakfast." Linda smiled and said nothing.

True to his word, George had a delicious breakfast waiting for the two of them. His face beamed as he came into the hall and took Linda's coat from Rick.

After breakfast, Rick and Linda walked into Rick's study and sat down. Rick was excited about something and Linda wondered what it was. He walked to the big window that took up almost one entire wall. As he returned to stand in front of her, he reached into his pocket and brought out a small box. He opened it and removed a platinum solitaire. It was the most beautiful diamond that Linda had ever seen. She stood breathless as he put it on her finger. She didn't say a word, but none was needed. The look she gave him was enough. Rick took care of the situation with a long, tender kiss. Linda was dizzy, and she wasn't sure whether it was the ring or the kiss. But it was all wonderful.

Standing there in the circle of his arms, she found her voice. "It's the most beautiful ring in the world! Oh, I love you so much, darling!"

When she looked at him, Rick suddenly thought of the stars back at the farm. They hadn't shone nearly so bright as the love in his sweetheart's eyes.

When they returned to Linda's tiny apartment, Rick was carrying several newspapers that told of their rescue. He had called the news office earlier to let them know that Linda was safe. He told Linda about it as they stepped into the elevator that would take them to her floor.

She made coffee as soon as they arrived and, sitting together in the booth, they read the news items that appeared. It was such fun, sitting here together. Linda thought how wonderful it would be when they were together forever.

After Rick left, the apartment seemed very empty. Linda cleaned up the coffee cups and tidied her apartment. Soon, she left to do some shopping. She would need a dress for the coming evening and she had other appointments.

Tonight's party would be an important occasion and Linda wanted to look just right. Rick wanted to announce their engagement. He thought it would be the perfect time and Linda wanted him to be proud of her. What a surprise their announcement would be! Neither of them said a word about their engagement to anyone except Linda's family. Just how big a surprise it would be, even Linda couldn't guess.

There was one person who was going to be very angry and she, in return, had a few surprises in store for Rick and Linda.

IX

Rick arrived right on time to take Linda to his apartment. He asked her to get there early so she could become familiar with all the rooms. He wanted her to feel relaxed and comfortable before the other guests arrived. Rick loved having her there. All the rooms seemed to take on a new brightness with Linda. Her presence delighted him, and he smiled to think that soon she would always be in his home. Rick stood smiling down at her now. She was so tiny that she only reached his heart.

"You look beautiful tonight, funny face," he teased her.

Linda blushed. Rick could not help but kiss the lovely color that stained her cheeks. He was so happy. He had found a beautiful woman and yet, in so many was, she was like an innocent little girl. Her dress was white velvet and when the lights fell on it, it shone with a deep luster. The tiny straps at the shoulders showed her tanned arms and throat to advantage. The tiny waist reached in and hugged her, and the skirt reached down to the tips of her white satin slippers.

George had taken their wraps and now he came toward them with drinks - cold and made just the way they liked them.

Before long, the guests started to arrive. The room was soon a loud mass of voices. Rick introduced Linda to the many celebrities, some of whom she had never met. At first, she felt ill at ease but, with Rick right beside her, she soon relaxed and started to enjoy the party.

When Rick was sure everyone had arrived, and they had all had a chance to tell Rick and Linda how lucky they had been to survive, he walked over to the musicians. With a gesture of his land, he stopped the music as though it had been prearranged.

Putting his arm around Linda, he said, "I want all of you to know that something very wonderful came from my ordeal. I have a very happy announcement to make." At his words, everyone started to crowd around.

"Linda has consented to become my wife, and we made it official today!"

As he said this, Rick lifted Linda's hand and the diamond sparkled. Although she was nervous at so much attention, Linda felt very proud. She held her hand there while the people gathered so close, admired the ring and congratulated them. There were stunned expressions in the room, and it was obvious to Linda that many of the women there had made some plans of their own for Rick's future.

In a few minutes, everyone started to go back to their drinks. The relief shone clearly on Linda's face when, suddenly she felt eyes staring at her. She lifted her head and looked straight into the hatred of a blond-haired girl. It was a look that made Linda's skin crawl. She knew his girl would be an enemy. But why?

Still puzzled, she watched the blonde girl walk toward them. Instinctively, Linda moved closer to Rick. The girl had been introduced to her earlier and she remembered the name. It was Carol. She turned her back to Linda and reached up and kissed Rick.

"Oh Rick! You had a nasty crack on the head! Don't you think an important decision like this should wait until you are feeling better?"

Everyone in the room stood like frozen statues. She had been talking so loudly, each person had heard it. Linda wished she could be swallowed up. She didn't know quite what to do.

Rick moved over to Linda and put his arm around her. When he spoke, his voice was low and calm. Linda, however, could tell that he was very angry. She waited to see what he would do.

"George, Miss Halliday is leaving. Will you please get her wrap and make sure she gets into a cab."

He had beckoned, and George was right there. It was almost a though they were used to her tantrums, Linda thought, as George walked Carol out the door.

Turning toward her now, Rick said, "Come on, honey, let's dance."

As they danced Rick whispered such nonsense to her that she was soon smiling, and the incident was almost forgotten.

Linda would find out later why the blonde, Carol, was so angry. Unfortunately, it would have an effect that would be much worse than tonight. For now, Linda brushed off the incident thinking that Carol was just another jealous woman. The rest of the evening went by in a happy blur of faces with much laughter and gaiety.

When the last of the guests had gone, Rick got her wrap and, dismissing George, said he would take her home himself. He asked Linda if she were too tired to talk for a while, and, wondering what was troubling him she said no.

When they arrived at her apartment, Rick came in and Linda made them some coffee. Again, Rick slid into the small booth in the kitchen and her apartment took on the glow of a real home. On an impulse, Linda reached over and kissed the dimple at the corner of Rick's mouth. The little brown imps started to dance deep in his eyes. Too late, she realized how much trouble an impulse like this could cause. He pulled her close to him and slowly kissed her. First her eyes, then her nose and finally his lips rested against her own. His kiss left her gasping and Linda slid out of the booth on the pretext that she wanted to refill their coffee cups. Although she trusted him implicitly, she wasn't so sure she trusted herself anymore. Not when her kissed her like that, anyway!

They talked about their wedding and other things for a while. Although he hated to, Rick finally told Linda about an engagement that would take him away from her for a week, the first of June. She knew that he had to go and although her heart ached at the thought, she answered as she knew she should.

"While you are gone, dear, I can visit my family. It will be for such a short time. I can get most of my wedding things made without any trouble. My aunt has a very good seamstress.

Rick knew how hard it would be for her staying behind while he left, and he admired her for trying to make it easier for him.

Linda was leaning in the circle of Rick's arms and he felt her stifle a yawn.

Lifting her from the booth, Rick said, "Off to bed with you, young lady." He smiled his sweet, gentle smile.

Linda stood, looking at the door, long after Rick left. She was thinking how lucky she was that he loved her. Although she was very tired, she roamed aimlessly around the apartment. She decided that maybe a warm bath would make her sleep.

Later, as she crawled into her bed, she tossed and turned for some time before sleep would come. When she finally did fall asleep, it was to have a horrible nightmare. Her dreams were of her mother. She could see her clearly and she seemed to be trying to tell Linda something. Linda could only hear an occasional word. It was as if the wind were blowing the words away.

"Be careful, dear. Don't let her hurt you."

That was all she could hear but the tears that were streaking her mother's cheeks alarmed her. She tried to answer her mother, but her voice wouldn't utter the words. She tried in vain. She could feel rain beating down and she was walking along a narrow, slippery path. Her dreams had become confused now and instead of her mother, it was Rick who was waiting at the end of the path. She couldn't get to him, no matter how hard she tried.

Linda awoke with a start. As she sat up in bed and turned on the light, she could feel the tears on her face. She looked at her little clock and saw it was past four. Opening the drawer by the side of her bed, Linda took out an old locket. Inside were two faded pictures. They were of her mother and father. The pictures were taken when her parents were first married. The faces that looked back at her were younger than she. She hadn't known them very long, but her aunt had talked about them so much that she felt very close to them.

Carefully, the troubled girl closed the locket and held it to her cheek. As though she had felt some small comfort from her action, Linda opened the drawer and replaced the locket where she found it. The familiar room felt cozy and her visions of Rick soon made her nightmare seem unreal and far away.

The gray morning was starting to break over the tall skyscrapers. Linda always enjoyed the tall buildings, standing like giant protectors. She sighed and settled down for another hour or two of sleep before she would have to go to work.

She overslept. It was late when she pulled her little roadster into her parking place. Hurrying into the office building, she hoped no one would notice her arrival. As she walked through the door, the first thing she saw was a huge bouquet of yellow roses sitting in the center of her desk. There was a card too, and it read, "Welcome home, Linda." Her friends from the office crowded around her and once more she had to tell her story. Sandy had run over and hugged her when she first came into the office. Then her eyes rested on the diamond. Leave it to Sandy. Linda had to repeat the story about her engagement to Rick and the girls looked at her with some envy when they heard who she was going to marry.

The only person there who was not surprised was Sandy. She was very happy; she knew how much her friend thought about this man even before the plane crash. She knew Linda. This would be the real love that she had looked for, for such a long time.

Later, there was a big cake to be eaten and even Mr. Weston come out to put his arm around Linda and tell her how happy he was to see her safely back home. Her eyes sparkled with unshed tears, but she managed to hold them back as she smiled and thanked all these good friends who wished her well.

After a while, things returned to normal and soon the office was humming with its usual number of things to check out and other activity. Linda and Sandy sat next to each other. They had an unusual number of things to talk about this day. Linda asked Sandy to be Maid of Honor at her wedding and Sandy was overjoyed.

As Linda left the office that evening, she was still feeling light and bubbly. Rick picked her up early and they drove along the shore road to watch the moon come up. They were too happy to share their love with anyone just yet. As they drove back to Linda's apartment later that evening, Rick noticed the troubled expression that crept onto her usually smiling face. She seemed reluctant to go inside. Rick decided to go in with her and maybe she would tell him what was wrong.

Finally, she could keep it to herself no longer and, little by little, the story of her nightmare came out. It was so good to have someone to talk to — someone who could understand. Linda sighed her relief. Rick did not want her to know how concerned he was. He was quite sure the nightmare had been brought on by Carol's behavior and it made him angry.

Instead of saying what he thought, Rick said, in his teasing way, "It's just the jitters, honey. Don't worry. Every bride gets them, I understand."

He was so funny that Linda soon found herself laughing at him. She loved him so much. She could not disguise it as she smiled at him now. Rubbing her cheek against the toughness of his jacket, Linda let her arms go around his neck and cling tightly.

He kissed her soft face and said, "It won't be long before we won't have to say goodnight anymore."

She kept her face against his jacket and nodded her head. She just wanted so much to stay close to him always.

That night there were no nightmares. Her fears had been forgotten and no ugly dreams came to haunt her sleep.

X

The next few weeks went by in a whirl of parties and showers for Linda. She and Sandy spent much time shopping. Rick had found a penthouse apartment which suited them both perfectly. They would be traveling most of the time, so they decided to buy one house on the coast and keep an apartment in New York. All too soon Rick was kissing her goodbye and she watched him step into the waiting jet. It would take him away from her for a week and Linda knew it would be the longest week of her life.

As she turned to walk back to the car, a face in the crowd looked vaguely familiar to Linda. It kept her troubled all the way home. Suddenly she remembered. It had been Carol's face she had seen. What was she doing at the airport? Linda decided that she had been mistaken. She started to think of something else, determined to put the incident out of her mind. Rick was right. She had a case of jitters all right! It was good for Linda to have something else to think about. She began deciding what to pack for her trip to Connecticut. Before she knew it, the car had stopped, and George was holding the door open for her to step out.

"Here we are, Miss." His formal voice made her smile.

As she stepped lightly from the car, Linda said, "George, I hope we will become good friends."

He returned her smile with a small salute of his cap and said, "I am sure we will! Mr. Morrow has excellent taste!"

Linda knew from his voice that he approved of her and it would be important because she had seen how carefully George attended to Rick's needs and how much Rick relied on his valet in return.

As she made her dinner, she found herself again thinking about George and she smiled at his attempt to make her feel comfortable, even though he was used to attending only to Rick's needs. She was certain she had won his approval.

Being very weary, Linda did her packing quickly and, after a tepid bath, she was ready for bed. It wasn't long before the small alarm was telling her, by its ringing, that it was time to get up. She arose and noticed the morning sun was just starting to stain the sky with its pink colors. She wanted to get an early start so, without waiting to make breakfast, she hurriedly dressed and started out.

Linda was wearing a yellow sundress, for the morning was warm and, with her dark hair cascading around her shoulders, she looked young and vulnerable. Her heart was filled with a deep contentment as she thought about her wonderful Rick. He was her whole world. In a very short time, she would be Mrs. Rickard Morrow. Smiling a little at the thought, Linda started humming a tune about a stranger. Her little car sped smoothly through the city traffic. Then onto the freeway. She had called Aunt Susan the day before and told her just about when to expect her arrival.

Aunt Susan was already bustling around as her husband sat watching her for a few minutes.

Then he said, "Come on, Sue. Sit down and have a second cup of coffee with me. There is plenty of time for whatever has to be done."

Mrs. O'Connor sat down at the kitchen table and rested as her husband brought her a coffee cup. He poured her coffee and watched as she sat drinking it thoughtfully. Her thoughts were on Linda, the girl they had raised from a child. She was their delight and they loved her dearly. God had been good to them. She talked quietly to her husband.

Then, as she finished her coffee, she remarked, "Oh, Edward, there are so many things to do before Linda arrives."

Her husband knew he had kept her with him for as long as he could and, as she hurried from the room, he watched her go with a smile of affection on his face. He didn't move from the table for some time. He was remembering back to when Linda was a small child. She had been his good companion. They had walked and talked together as though they were father and daughter. Joy was mirrored in the man's seamed and weathered face. He was thinking now of Linda's coming marriage. He had liked Rick the minute he first saw him. He felt a sudden happiness that Linda had found someone like Rick to take care of her. Slowly, he arose from his chair, still with the small smile on his face, and went outside to start filling the pool for his girl.

For some reason, Mrs. O'Connor removed the lovely yellow spread from Linda's bed and the curtains from her window. She went to a cedar chest in the attic and carried a beautiful, frothy white spread and curtains to Linda's room.

She handled them gently and there was a mist in her eyes that she would never be able to explain. When she had finished, the room no longer belonged to a young girl. Now it was a woman's room. The white spread and curtains belonged to Linda's mother. It had been on her parents' bed the day they died. Her aunt had promised that she would have these things at the proper time. Somehow, now seemed like the very day! The room was transformed. All that remained was the green rug with the yellow splashes, and the green and yellow pillows.

As she stood back and looked about the room, Aunt Susan could almost see again the young couple who had once occupied this very room. The warmth of their long-ago love filled the room.

A gentle breeze ruffled the curtains and, just as the gray-haired woman turned to leave the room, Uncle Edward walked in with an armful of yellow roses.

"It's almost as though they were here, Mother," he said softly as he slipped the roses into a vase on the little pie-shaped table which stood by Linda's favorite chair.

"Yes, it is," she agreed, and, with a gentle sigh, she rubbed her hand across the spread. When they reached the hallway below Aunt Susan's eye caught the gleam of sun shining on the pool just beyond the patio. He husband had been busy too, she thought now, as she looked lovingly at him.

He had put the patio furniture out. Everything was ready for Linda's visit. She had been so anxious that everything be just right that she hadn't realized just how important this visit was to her husband.

Although the beach was just a few steps away, Linda loved her pool best. She often went out there to think or to concentrate on her writing. The beach was fine for picnics and large gatherings, but the pool was perfect for the quiet times. Linda's aunt smiled as the words went through her mind. How often she had heard Linda say that very thing.

Just then, she heard the unmistakable sound of a motor coming up the long driveway. Happily, she hurried to the front hall. She and her husband stood on the large front porch together and watched the snappy little sports car come up the drive.

Linda stepped lightly from the car and ran up the steps to her waiting family. He aunt and uncle received her as only a loving family could. The two women walked into the house together and Uncle Ed went to get the bags and carry them to Linda's room. Linda had never looked more radiant, he noticed as he watched her graceful movements.

"It is so good to be home," Linda said.

As she looked at the two people who were so dear to her, her heart ached a little. She noticed that they were starting to age and, for some reason, that made her sad. She hated to see them grow old. She loved them so much! How lucky she had been to have someone like them to love her.

After lunch they sat on the big old-fashioned porch that looked down to the water's edge. Aunt Susan had jealously turned her kitchen over to the maid. Linda smiled at the many times the maid had arrived only to find most of the work already done.

105

The day flew by, filled with happiness and laughter. Driving in the hot sun had made Linda sleepy and by nine o'clock she was yawning. She kissed her happy aunt and uncle goodnight and went to her room. When she closed her bedroom door, she noticed for the first time that Aunt Susan had made some changes. She could feel the difference in herself and now she was sure her aunt had noticed it too. She was going to be married and, being in love made her so happy.

With her eyes closed and her head resting against the coolness of the mantle, Linda let herself think of Rick. She loved the way his eyes teased; she loved the dimples he always tried to hide. The thought of becoming his wife made her breath catch deep down inside her. A thrill shot through her at the memory of his touch.

Slowly, she came back to the present and decided to get ready for bed. She took a hot bath and, after putting on a long yellow gown that floated behind her as she walked, Linda came back to sit before the mirror and brush her long hair – the hair Rick loved to touch. She sat for a long time brushing her hair until it shone in the soft light. Afterward, Linda turned off the lights and went to stand by the big window. The soft light breeze came in to caress her face.

The moon was bathing the whole world with its pale glow and, as she looked down at the shimmering beach, she whispered to the night, "I love you Rick. Please, hurry home to me."

With tender thoughts of her love still glowing inside her, it wasn't long until she was fast asleep.

XI

Linda opened her eyes to the most beautiful morning she had ever seen. It was still early so she stayed there and quietly enjoyed the fresh breeze that was coming through the open window. The air was so clean and fresh after the cinder-filled city air – so much nicer.

This is the perfect time for a swim," she thought as she got out of bed quickly.

Dressed in a white tank suit, she ran silently down the stairs and out the kitchen door.

The water was cold and brisk, and Linda swam as fast as she could across the pool and back again.

"It really keeps me moving," she laughed to herself.

Before very long she began to enjoy the water. She had exercised enough so that she was warm now.

Then she saw a red flash come through the hedge from the house next door. She looked up and exclaimed in a startled voice, "Carol! What are you doing here?"

It wasn't very nice to say but, somehow, Carol looked very out of place in the country.

"Let me in the pool and I'll tell you," Carol replied in a teasing voice.

This girl could be very likeable when she wanted to be, Linda decided.

"Of course! Come on in."

Linda wasn't really that happy to have company but, she was too well-mannered to be rude to anyone. With so much happiness to share, she felt very generous.

They swam around for a while, talking about the changes in the Connecticut countryside.

Then Linda asked again, "Just what are you doing here, Carol?"

"Oh, I am visiting some friends this week. They invited me to come and, here I am! You know the Bensons, don't you?" Carol answered slyly.

She knew very well that Linda knew the Bensons. They had been next door neighbors since Linda could remember.

"Is that who you are staying with?" Linda asked, after a very long pause.

It seemed strange that Carol knew these people, and yet Linda had never seen her there before.

"They are wonderful people," she added, not wanting to sound too cold.

After swimming around in silence for a while, Linda invited Carol to stay for breakfast. She introduced Carol to her aunt and uncle and then showed her into the dining room.

Although Aunt Susan was cordial to Carol, Linda sensed that her aunt did not like the girl.

Her uncle just grunted a, "How do you do," and out he went.

It would be hard to tell just what he did think without asking outright.

After breakfast, Carol suggested that Linda ride into the nearby city to do some shopping for small items they both needed. Thinking it might be fun to have someone her own age to talk to, Linda agreed. They went off happily, leaving the older people to linger over their coffee together. As they left the room, Linda noticed a worried frown on her aunt's face. Her uncle looked concerned for some reason as well.

Linda went back and kissed them both good bye on an impulse she did not quite understand.

At lunch time, Carol insisted on treating Linda to lunch. By now, Linda was beginning to feel a little silly for distrusting Carol back in New York. She was being so sweet. They spent the entire afternoon shopping. Linda knew her aunt would not expect her before dinner time. Thoroughly exhausted, the two girls started home. They chatted happily about their purchases and what they had seen in the different shops. Being a thoroughly sly person, Carol never mentioned the coming marriage. Linda thought it strange but was shy about mentioning it herself.

In a short while they arrived home. Linda walked through the open kitchen door. The smell of food made her realize how hungry she was.

"Run upstairs and wash dear. Dinner is ready, "Aunt Susan greeted her.

"Okay! I'll be right down "Linda answered as she ran up the stairs singing under her breath.

Her aunt stood watching her with a frown on her pretty face. She did not like this Carol. Where had she come from? Aunt Susan had never seen her at the Bensons before.

If she had only known the truth, it would have saved everyone a lot of heartache. She had mentioned this girl to her husband just that morning. He laughed at her uneasy feeling.

After dinner, which was a delightful occasion, the three people sat together in the drawing room with their coffee. Uncle Edward retired behind his paper. Aunt Susan was knitting, and Linda just sat sipping her coffee, lost in happy dreams. It had been a busy day and soon the beautiful old house sat dark and quiet.

Aunt Susan's dreams were dark and fearful that night – as though a dark shadow was hanging over their home. She tossed and murmured fitfully in her sleep.

The next two days the girls were constantly together - swimming, shopping or just talking. Carol ate dinner with the O'Connors on Wednesday night. After they finished eating the older couple went to the drawing room for coffee. The two girls took their coffee outside by the pool. Carol didn't seem to be in any great hurry to leave so they lingered until late. Sometimes they spoke of mutual friends but mostly they just relaxed, each in their comfortable chair, and dreamed their private daydreams.

Finally, Carol spoke. Her voice, in the deep stillness, startled Linda, jolting her back to the present.

"I'm sorry, Carol. What did you say?"

"I thought it might be fun to take the motor boat out tomorrow. Maybe we could go on a picnic," Carol repeated.

For just a moment, Linda felt a cold chill run through her.

"How silly I am," she thought. Turning to her companion, she said, "Of course! I would love it. Where would you like to go?"

"Oh, the very best place is the island," Carol answered blandly.

Again, the icy fingers gripped at Linda's heart. She shook herself mentally.

"Fine, let's leave at ten. It will be warm, and we can have a nice day exploring the island."

With everything decided for the next day, they said goodnight, and each went their own way.

As Linda entered the house, she went in search of her aunt to tell her about the plans for the next day. The maid told her that her aunt and uncle had retired early. They, too, were leaving early the next morning and they would be gone all day.

Feeling a little upset, Linda decided she would get up early so she could talk to them. For some reason, it seemed very important to her to let them know where she was going.

When she fell asleep, Linda dreamed of Rick. She could see him in the distance but no matter how she tried, she could not reach him. He neither saw her nor did he hear her calling his name. After a while, he disappeared from her sight. Linda was so frightened that she awoke sobbing as though her heart would break.

She sat on the wide window seat and looked down at the quiet, deserted beach. This was the second time she had dreamed like this. She felt a little silly for having been so afraid. Rick would be her in just three more days. She hugged her knees and dreamed of how wonderful it would be when he arrived.

At the thought of his dark, handsome, face, and the way his lips would make her forget everything, her cheeks burned.

"I love you Rick. Please, hurry home to me," she said aloud as she looked up at the dark velvet sky. The moon was beginning to dip low as Linda slipped back into bed. Her dream was forgotten.

XII

Carol had been very angry when Rick and Linda had announced that they would be married. She made no secret to any of her friends that she fully intended to marry Rick again, herself. In fact, she had given the hands-off sign to all female members of her set. She used every method she could think of to get him back, but he had not been even lukewarm to her coy efforts.

She had been such a fool to give him up in the first place. It had been a terrible mistake.

"Couldn't Rick understand that?" she asked herself over and over.

She had been so sure he was going to start taking her out again. Then this girl had to come along.

"Where did she come from anyway," she angrily asked herself, then, through clenched teeth, she vowed, "I will find a way to get him from her."

There was nothing pretty about her expression now.

She started to plan – first one way, then another – to break up the happy young couple. Carol knew that Rick had not told Linda about her. That would make it much easier for her to find a way. She decided the first thing she must do was to make friends with this little intruder. Carol set about at once being very charming whenever Linda was around. She even made a big occasion of giving a shower for her coming wedding. Finally, she began to see that Linda was starting to trust her and she even seemed to like her. At least, she told herself this was so.

They could never be close friends, but this was good enough for what Carol planned. The day came when she heard that Rick was going out of town for a week. This would be her chance. With Rick around, there would never be an opportunity to get rid of his simpering girlfriend; this much she knew.

She still wasn't sure how to accomplish her plan, but it had to be now. She would never have a better chance.

As soon as Carol heard that Linda was going to Connecticut, she contacted a friend – a woman she had met just a short time before in New York. They had invited her to visit them sometime after she insisted that she just loved he country. They had offered the invitation in an offhand way and then forgot about it. They were very surprised to hear her voice when she called that day.

"Hello, Mrs. Benson. This is Carol Halliday. I wonder if this weekend would be convenient for me to visit? I really need to get away for a few days and a friend of mine is going to be nearby."

It was obvious she would be hard to say no to, so Mrs. Benson said they would be delighted to have her.

"Thank you, Mrs. Benson. I will see you this weekend," Carol trilled as she hung up the phone.

She did a dance step around the room and chanted to herself.

"So far, so good!"

Now she would start getting the proper clothes ready and pack. She wore a vicious, cruel smile on her bitter face.

Carol arrived right on schedule. The Bensons were still a little stunned by the invasion but, remembering her as a pleasant girl, they welcomed her cordially.

She knew the Bensons lived right next door to Linda's family, so she was careful not to mention that she knew Linda. Everything was planned – right to the last detail. She wanted to make sure that nothing went wrong. It was so easy!

Linda accepted her presence without questions. She even seemed grateful for this young company. Carol had counted on that. The Bensons were so much older, they would hardly make conversation with someone so much younger than themselves. In her selfish mind, Carol could not understand how Linda could love her aunt and uncle so much or that with love comes understanding.

Having Carol there posed no problem for the Bensons. They just went on with their schedule, at Carol's urging, and they were delighted to have a house guest who so obviously wanted to entertain herself.

When Carol met Linda's aunt and uncle, she felt their instant dislike for her, but she had no intention of letting two old people stand in her way. She knew she would have some trouble getting them to accept her. But she also relied on the fact that their love for their niece would prevent them from keeping her away if Linda wanted her around.

She decided to spend as much time as possible with Linda and win her over completely before she put her plan into action.   She waited until she was sure before she suggested a picnic.

Carol was elated at her success when Linda agreed so quickly. As she fell asleep that night, Carol murmured to herself, "Tomorrow it will be all over. He will be mine again. He belongs to me and no one else will have him. No one will ever take him away from me again."

XIII

Rick had dreaded this trip. He wouldn't ever leave Linda behind him again. The silver jet slid quietly through the night. The valet brought his tray and a bottle of champagne.

"Bring your tray and sit with me, George," Rick suggested.

It was not unusual for the two men to sit together for meals. They had a friendship that went back a long way. Rick knew that George approved of Linda. George never said so in words, but he let Rick know by his actions whom he did or did not approve of. Carol was one person Rick's valet had never liked. She was always "Ma'am," and never "Mrs. Morrow" to George. Carol had treated him as a servant, always looking down her nose at him. He was never a servant in Rick's mind. Carol had tried several times to fire him, but Rick had always intervened, and George stayed on.

The two men ate their dinner and discussed the week that lay ahead. All that week, as Rick went onto the stage, his only thought was to get this week finished so he could get home to the girl he loved. Her lovely face was constantly floating before him. Wednesday night, Rick performed as usual, but for some reason, he felt jittery. It was so unlike him.

"I'll call Linda right after the performance," he decided.

On trips like this, he always looked forward to seeing and talking to his fans, but tonight everything annoyed him. He tried not to be rude or impolite, but he was glad when he finally signed the last autograph and shook the final hand for that night.

As soon as he reached his room he tried to call Linda. All through the late hours he tried but to no avail. He could not get through. George, who was always calm, was beginning to worry about Rick. Rick had given him a job when he needed it so desperately and he, in return, gave his complete loyalty.

Finally, Rick decided it was useless to try any longer. He could not get through.

He turned to George and said, "I must go home tomorrow. I will have to get someone to replace me here for the last two performances."

Reaching for the phone, it wasn't long until he lined up a friend who could replace him, saying that he would be very happy to do it. George was already packing and checking on the next flight to New York. He was able to get Rick on a flight that would leave the next afternoon. Rick knew he could always depend on George for anything.

123

I'll fly to New York, pick up the car, and drive to Connecticut," Rick thought.

Now, with a smile, he anticipated Linda's surprise when he arrived early. Still smiling, and with a lighter heart, Rick showered and, after a few last details, decided to go to bed early. Before he fell asleep, he vowed to himself that in the future wherever he entertained, Linda would be in the audience where he could see her.

Rick's flight left right on time the following day. He knew he would be late getting to the O'Connor's house, but he could make it by eight thirty and that would be early enough so that he and Linda could still have time for a good talk.

He thought of the Casino he had just left behind. He remembered the heavy velvet tapestry, deep red in color, and the sprays of lights that made dining so intimate. He thought of his act that had brought him overnight popularity. He would give it all right now for a glance at the girl he loved so very much. Not being able to contact her by phone the night before had kept this need close to the surface of his mind. He wondered how he ever could have thought he loved Carol. He had never real known what love was. Strange, that a man could have so much experience with life and know as many women as he had known, without ever really falling in love.

124

Finally, Rick saw the familiar lights of the runway just beneath him. He had to fight his impatience as he waited for the cab to deliver him to his apartment. He had left George behind to take care of all final details and to follow later. They would meet in New York.

He backed a speedy little sportscar from the apartment garage and into the evening traffic. His mind ticked off the time. Just two more hours and he would be there. He stopped at the first service station he came to for gas and cigarettes. Thinking how long two hours could be, he decided to call and let Linda know he was on his way. He dialed the phone and waiting for what seemed an eternity. Finally, the click at the other end told him someone was answering.

"Hello! Hello, Linda? Is that you, dear?" Rick asked hopefully.

"No. This is Mrs. O'Connor. Oh Rick! Where are you?" The voice at the other end of the phone had a note of panic.

"I'm here in New York, Aunt Susan. Why? Is something wrong?"

Now it was Rick's turn to feel worried.

Mrs. O'Connor sighed. "Linda has been gone all day. She was supposed to be home for dinner, but she hasn't come home yet."

She went on to tell him that Linda had left a note saying she would go on a picnic that day with her friend, Carol, but to expect her in time for dinner.

"Oh no!" Rick moaned the worlds. "Did you say Carol, Aunt Susan?"

Rick's voice begged her to say no but he had heard right. Knowing that he must not frighten the older lady, Rick quickly replaced the note in his voice with one of optimism. He spoke to her in a cheerful way now.

"Don't worry, Aunt Susan. I am sure Linda is fine. I will be there soon."

He made the conversation short as possible without acting anxious, even though he could hardly wait to get on his way. He said goodbye and hurried out to his car. There was no time to waste.

Without Linda, life would be nothing. She had taught him the meaning of love. Her shy smile, her dainty ways, her funny little dignified expression. Even now, as worried as he was, a tiny smile tugged at the corner of his mouth.

Coming back to the present, he shuddered, "Oh God! Why didn't I tell her about Carol? If anything happens it will be all my fault!" Rick was really praying, "Please, God. She has been through so much because of me. Don't let anything happen to her."

He remembered how vicious Carol was and how easy it would be for her to trap a gentle little person like Linda.

Rick hurried on through the night. It had grown windy and the rain was starting to fall. It seemed to Rick as though the miles stretched on without end.

"Of course," he argued to himself, "I am just doing a lot of worrying for nothing. She will be there when I arrive. I will walk through the door and I will feel her arms, and breathe in the smell of her perfume."

His thoughts continued. "I will hear her say, 'I love you, Rick,' with the same wonder that I feel each time I say it to her."

After what seemed an eternity, Rick turned off the highway and soon was driving through the winding land, onto the driveway. The lights of the house beckoned with a welcome glow.

"She will be there. She must be there." It was all he could think.

XIV

Linda awoke to the startling brightness of the morning sun.

"Oh, dear," she sighed as she scrambled out of bed, "It must be very late."

Picking up her robe, she headed for the hall. "Aunt Susan, are you there?

Her anxious voice floated through the silent house. Somehow, she sensed that her aunt and uncle had left, and she knew the servants had the day off. She felt very alone in the big, old house.

Shrugging her shoulder and trying to be nonchalant, she murmured to herself, "I will just have to leave a note."

She was fully awake now and felt silly for her momentary fear. This was her home. She could never feel anything but safe here. Satisfied, Linda walked to the pantry just off the kitchen and started getting things ready for the picnic. One thing she had learned about Carol in a very short time was that she was an absolute scatter-brain.

Even though the picnic was Carol's idea, she would no doubt show up empty handed.

"Oh well! There's plenty here."

Linda smiled and, nodding her head, carried her coffee cup to the table. As she sat at the table, drinking her coffee, she made sandwiches and started putting them into an old basket she had pulled from the shelf when she first entered the pantry. Linda worked quietly and quickly in the stillness of the kitchen.

Her thoughts suddenly strayed to Rick.

"Soon I will be seeing him again and when he comes home this time, he will stay. If he should have to go anywhere again, I can go with him." Her thoughts ran on, "How wonderful it will be to see him each morning when I open my eyes."

"Oh Rick," she said aloud, "I love you."

At that very moment Carol opened the kitchen door.

"Hello, Linda," she cried gaily, pretending she had not heard what Linda had just been saying.

She tried to keep a friendly smile on her face, but the hate bubbled very closed to the surface.

"You are just in time to join me for more coffee, Carol," Linda said, wondering if her earlier words had carried as far as the door.

They had coffee and talked about the beautiful weather and soon it was time to leave. Linda hated to leave the peaceful, warm feeling of the kitchen.

"This is silly," she thought. Linda mentally shook herself and picked up the picnic basket.

"I will meet you at the boat, Carol. I must check the front of the house," Linda called.

She wanted to be alone when she wrote her note. It was short. It said only, "Dear Aunt Susan, Carol and I are going on a picnic. I will be home for dinner. Love, Linda."

With a lighter heart, she headed for the beach and Carol. Her friend seemed very impatient.

"Come on, Linda! It's getting late," she called as Linda made her way down the steps to the beach. Soon everything was in the little outboard that her uncle enjoyed so very much. It was tied to a tiny pier along with a very old and awkward row boat.

Linda tried to row the boat many times, but it was much too heavy for her to handle. The girls untied the small craft and soon they were on their way. As they sped toward the island, they made idle chatter, although neither girl really seemed to have her mind on what she was saying. Carol seemed to be in unusually high spirits and laughed at the smallest, dullest remarks.

Linda mentioned it to her, but Carol brushed it off saying, "It's such a glorious day and I feel so happy! Do you know, Linda, I feel as though all of my dreams could come true today!"

Linda was smiling by now because Carol had such a truly happy expression on her face. She hoped that Carol had as much happiness as she, herself, did.

Carol changed the subject abruptly. It snatched Linda back from her thoughts and nudged her into the present. Immediately she noticed that Carol was suddenly acting very strange. Linda found herself wishing they had never started out on this picnic. She shivered as though a chill wind was blowing over her.

"This is foolish, "she thought to herself. "I am just being jittery. The Island has always made me feel this way." Her thoughts raced on even though she knew it wasn't so. She loved this island.

Just then, they pulled into the cove. Linda had no more time to think or worry. Jumping out, she tied the boat securely. Carol let the motor die. Then she, too, jumped to the shore. They headed toward a small path that ran from the shore upward. The path had become overgrown because so few trips were made there anymore. Linda's parents had owned the island as had her grandparents before them. Now, it belonged to Linda. She hoped that someday she and Rick might restore some of the old building.

The girls reached a grassy knoll and dropped down to rest for a moment. The view of the water was magnificent. The grass beneath them was like a lush green carpet. The foliage looked like emerald green velvet as it hung over them, providing cool shade.

132

Carol broke into Linda's thoughts.

"Come on, slowpoke! Let's leave this lovely place."

Slowly, Linda got up from where she had been sitting and led the way silently thought the dark green coolness of the path. She was so proud of this island, and she wished now with all her heart that she had brought Rick here first. She would have liked to have him see all the places she had played as a child. This is where she had come for weekends when she visited her grandparents. She loved them so much! Even though they had died shortly after her parents, she could remember coming here to play and dream.

All at once, the dark green trees gave way to a large clearing and right in the center was the big house where her grandparents had lived. The place stood there in the filtering sunlight, looking so lonely with its loose shingles, broken steps and shutters, so in need of repair.

Once more, Linda thought of Rick.

"He could do so much here," she thought, "with all of his marvelous ideas!"

He was so creative! Linda was already looking forward to fixing the inside as well as the outside. Just the thought sent her spirits soaring.

"This was my grandparents' house, Carol," she said quietly.

With an impatient edge, Carol urged, "Well, let's go in!"

She was already up the steps. For some reason, Linda did not want Carol inside the house. She stepped in front of the other girl and remarked, "I'm sorry but the door is locked, and I did not bring my key."

Carol did not even argue, much to Linda's surprise. She just headed for the path that led around the corner of the house.

Over her shoulder, she called to Linda, "I see some beautiful plants by the small shed back here! Would it be all right if I dig one for Mrs. Benson?"

Linda replied without hesitation, "Of course! I'm sure she would enjoy having it."

She was standing beside Carol now.

"What can I use to dig with, Linda?" The pale, slim girl looked so helpless.

"Just a minute. There should be something in the storage shed."

As Linda said it, she could not help laughing. Carol certainly would never make a gardener; she was sure of that!

Stepping into the shed, she started to look for a spade, feeling sure there would be one someplace inside. Suddenly, the door slammed shut. Linda stood trembling in the complete darkness. She felt the panic starting to rise inside her.

"Carol! Carol," she called. "Please help me. The door seems to be stuck."

For the first time, she noticed that Carol had not uttered one word on the other side of the door. Now she knew why she had felt such a reluctance to come here with this girl. Carol was trying to harm her. But for what reason?

She was locked in here. Just as this thought reached her, she heard the bar scrape across the outside of the door. She really was locked in. Trapped!

"What will I do," she whispered.

She tried the door again.

"Carol? Please let me out!" Her pleading voice fell on deaf ears. The only answer she heard was a wild laughter.

"You won't ever get out, Linda," the voice sneered. "You will never see your Rick again. Until you came along he was mine! And now he will belong to me again. I will make him forget all about you!"

Again, Linda heard the horrible laugh, followed by the sound of footsteps rustling down the path. She realized that there was something very wrong with Carol's mind and that this was why she had felt so uneasy today. It just didn't register before. Now it was too late.

"Oh God! What am I going to do? How will I ever get out of here? No one will ever know where I am."

She was very frightened now. She pushed and tugged on the heavy door until she was exhausted.

"If only it wasn't so dark," she thought. There were no windows in the shed. "Thank heavens for the small cracks! They will let in the light."

Her busy mind continued. It was lucky she didn't realize how little air there was in the shed and that, without those cracks, she would suffocate.

Finally, Linda managed to calm herself. She knew she must conserve her strength. Sitting on a small watering can that was turned upside down on the old wooden floor, her mind went back to what Carol had been saying.

"Why? Why had she done this? What had Carol been raving about?"

Linda was sure it had something to do with Rick. But what? Either Carol's mind had become completely unhinged or she was in love with him. Or could it be a little of both?

Linda knew that Rick had never paid any special attention to Carol. The only time Carol had said anything was the night Rick announced their engagement. She was remembering now, how worried and embarrassed she had been that night.

What had given Carol the right to do such a thing?

"Oh, Rick! If only you could hear me. I need you so much."

The thought that he might never hear her again was too much for her tired mind. She cried until there were no more tears to be shed.

After a while, she started to pace the small area again.

"What a fool I was! Carol had planned this all along and I played right into her hands. If only I had talked to Aunt Susan first," She thought tiredly. "They will never think to look here for me."

The tears started to flow again, but Linda didn't even try to brush them away this time. She noticed that light was not coming through the cracks now. It had started to rain, and the wind was making the old building creak. Linda felt very hungry; she thought of the lunch down by the water where they had left it. Dinner would be over by now and her family would start to worry about her. Linda sat on the hard floor and rested her head on the water can. She thought of all the wonderful plans she and Rick had made. Her wonderful, darling Rick! So much happiness for two people. Was it really too much to ask? As her mind continued to work, her love for him overwhelmed her and the sobs started again. Finally, she fell asleep, too exhausted to think any more.

~ ~ ~

As Carol walked away from the shed, which she had locked securely, with Linda inside, she was muttering to herself.

"There! I have succeeded! She is gone! And Rick is mine again."

Her confused mind just kept the one thought. It never occurred to her that anyone would even look for Linda.

If anyone had taken a careful look at Carols' action the past few months, they would have seen the change. Where she had been merely a selfish, willful girl, her mind had become cunning. If Rick had seen her he would have noticed the bitter hatred she had for anyone who looked his way. She could be sweet and charming when she chose to be, but vicious if anyone crossed her. The only people who had even guessed at this had been Linda's aunt and uncle. Carol had been clever enough never to show that side of her in front of Rick. He would have seen through her in a second. He had seen her at her very worst!

When she discovered that Rick would be away, and that Linda would be going to Connecticut, Carol decided that the timing would be perfect. She had even gleaned information about Linda's childhood from the unsuspecting Bensons. They had known Linda since she was born. When her parents died, they cared for her until the O'Connors could come for her. Linda was like a relative to them. And it was from the Bensons that Carol found out about the island.

Carol was hysterical and very unstable by the time she reached the boat. It has started to rain. She'd been wandering around for some time, unable to find her way. In her hurry to get away from the shed, she had missed the path that led to the water's edge and became lost in the woods. It had grown quite dark now too. Carol had very little experience with boats, so it took her a while to get the engine started. It was Linda who had started it when they left the beach; Carol never thought of how she would get back when her plans were made.

Finally, the little boat obeyed her, and she started across the water. The winds were gusting now, and the water was very rough. Carol swung the wheel too sharply and a heavy wave struck directly against the side of the light boat. It tipped over, spilling the frightened girl into the water. Carol could swim, but this day had been too much for her. She panicked. She flailed her arms but, not being very strong, it wasn't long until she gasped and disappeared into the dark, murky water.

XV

Uncle Edward parked in the driveway.

"It's been a long day, dear," he said as he opened the door for his wife.

"A cup of tea and we will feel as good as new," she replied, patting his cheek.

The love between these two people was a beautiful sight for anyone to behold.

"Linda must be in the kitchen, mother," the man stated.

Without waiting for an answer, he led the way to the kitchen door. The house seemed very empty to the couple as they closed the door behind them. Aunt Susan called to her niece, but only the echo of her own voice answered her. She climbed the stairs to check Linda's room, thinking she might be asleep. It was unlike Linda not to have a warm dinner waiting for them. Aunt Susan started back down the stairs with a worried frown on her face. As she reached the landing at the foot of the stairs, Uncle Edward came toward her. He had a white sheet of paper in his hand; it was a note. His face wore a strained expression.

"Mother, she went on a picnic, and she said to expect her home for dinner. It is strange that she hasn't arrived by now," he continued with a gesture.

Just then the phone rang. With a look of relief, Aunt Susan hurried to answer it, with a breathless, "That must be her now, Ed."

She picked up the phone.

Before she could say a word, the voice on the other end was saying, "Linda, Linda! Is that you?"

"That was Linda's young man, dad. He is on the way here," his wife explained, hanging up the phone.

"I am sure everything will be fine now. Rick will take care of everything," she continued hopefully.

They walked back to the kitchen, still uneasy but feeling better just knowing Rick would soon arrive.

Dinner was a quiet meal for the O'Connors and they ate very little. Trying to keep the conversation light so as not to upset the other, each one tried to think about where Linda might be.

The wind was starting to rattle the shutters and a soft patter of rain was falling. It was growing dark when a car came down the lane and pulled into the winding driveway.

As Rick jumped from his car, he noticed the lights in the kitchen. He opened the heavy door and stepped into the hall, unannounced. The O'Connors came hurrying into the front hall.

"Oh Rick! We are so glad you are here," Aunt Susan cried.

"She couldn't have gone far, Aunt Susan," the tall, dark-haired man assured her, his arm around her comfortingly. He read, then re-read, the note. Linda never broke a promise. He knew something must be wrong.

Not wanting to upset the worried couple, Rick hesitated to suggest calling the police.

"I think I will walk along the beach. Is there any special place she might go for a picnic," Rick inquired?

"Oh yes. Let me go with you," Uncle Ed said. "Mother, you wait here in case Linda should come home."

The two men started out into the stormy night.

"I'm worried, Rick," the older man stated.

"Yes sir, so am I." Rick decided to be honest with Mr. O'Connor.

He felt it would be easier to search if they could speak freely to each other. The men walked slowly along the beach and, as they walked, they called out to Linda. Only the echo of their own voices came back on the wind.

"I know Linda would have been in touch with us by now if she could," Uncle Ed stated flatly. "What do you suppose could have happened, Rick," the older man asked, concern on his face showing plainly.

Rick reached out and touched Uncle Ed on the shoulder.

"We will find her, Mr. O'Connor. I love her too much to lose her now." His voice had grown husky as he spoke, and it was easy to see how very much he cared.

Just then, Rick spotted something white further down the beach. His heart was racing, and he felt despair as he had never known it before. He started running and, fully clothed, went into the water. It was an overturned boat. Pulling it onto the beach, he saw the letters painted on the side: LUCKY LINDA.

Turning around, he saw that no words were needed. Uncle Edward was as white as the boat he was staring at. The look of complete horror on his face pulled Rick from his own fear-filled thoughts.

"It may have broken loose from the mooring," he suggested, half-heartedly.

The two men hurried to the small pier. They both knew at once that the boat had been untied and had not just broken loose as they had hoped.

"Try to think, Uncle Edward," Rick was using the name without even realizing it. "Why would they take the boat out?" Rick was so worried now that he spoke abruptly in a hoarse voice.

Linda's uncle understood how Rick must be feeling and he could not be offended. He, too, felt as though something dreadful had happened to his niece. As he stood there, looking at the pier, he knew why they had used the boat. His voice was shaking with excitement as he turned to Rick.

"The island," he exclaimed! "I know where they went, Rick! The only place in the world Linda would have gone on a picnic with the boat is to the island."

Rick started up the beach to the motor boat but, after he dragged it out, he saw that the motor had been damaged and that it would be of no use to him. He stood there for a moment trying to decide what to do.

Then, deciding that Mr. O'Connor had had just about enough excitement, he suggested in a matter-of-fact tone, "Sir, you go back to the house and call the police. Tell them what we know and what you think may have happened. Ask them to assist us in the search for the girls. Check with Mr. and Mrs. Benson to see if Carol has returned. It is possible that both girls are there, and we are worrying needlessly."

"What are you going to do, Rick," Uncle Ed asked, as both men stood in the rain, drenched through and not even noticing it.

Rick answered without wasting a word. "I am going to the island."

Uncle Ed looked at him in dismay.

"Son, all we have is the rowboat and it will never get you that far. It's rough going out there and you are not used to rowing."

He knew, even as he spoke, that he may as well save his words. The young man did not even hear him.

Rick was already on his knees, struggling with the rope that held the rowboat secure. It was a good, heavy rowboat and the oars were built for heavy duty use. They would get a workout this night; Rick was sure of that. He was glad they were securely attached to the boat with heavy rings. He lowered himself slowly into the boat and, looking out over the dark water, he headed in the direction to which Uncle Edward had pointed.

XVI

The going was very slow. Rick was not used to rowing, just as Uncle Ed had said. It wasn't long before his hands were raw and bleeding. He didn't even notice this; he was busy thinking back.

"I'm certain Carol is behind all this. I'll deal with her if she harms Linda." He spoke aloud to the wind.

There was no room for anything except thoughts of Linda - if she were all right, if only she would be found safe. He ached with the thought. He wondered where she was and if she was in a warm place.

"She is so small and fragile," he thought to himself, anxiously. "This storm would be too much for her."

Rick's heart was filled with his love. He knew now why he had felt the need to come home. He loved her so desperately! All Rick could think of was the feel of her soft round arms and the sweetness of her kisses. He remembered the loneliness that had filled his days before he met her – his Linda. A surge of determination poured through him, giving him a new strength. With renewed effort, he pulled on the awkward oars. He could feel tears of frustration.

150

As though in answer to his prayer, a strong wind started blowing against his back. Someone's hand seemed to be guiding him as he rowed straight for the island. The night was so dark, and the rain beat down so hard, that Rick did not realize that his boat was heading for the little cove. He knew only that Linda just had to be safe. There was no life without her. Rick could not even think of a future without the girl who had changed his whole life.

He remembered how courageous she had been in Maine. "What a girl," he thought to himself.

Her determination would see her through again; he was sure of it. Hanging tightly to this thought, Rick bent low over the oars and strained against the swirling waters.

With a start, Rick came back to the present. He boat had moved into the little cove and bumped against the shore. Gratefully, he jumped out and, struggling with the heavy boat, managed to pull it to higher ground. Reaching into his pocket, he found the flashlight Aunt Susan had handed him when he left the house to search the beach.

The trees made the night seem darker here on the island. He scrambled up the path, made muddy by the rain. He was slipping and sliding but somehow, with the aid of the wet branches, he made some headway. The branches reached out and drenched him until he felt sure he could get no wetter.

As Rick reached the knoll, his flashlight picked out a bright yellow gleam. He bent down and picked it up. It was one of Linda's ribbons; he knew it instinctively. As he knelt there, holding the ribbon to his cheek, a vision of her blue eyes, bright with mischief, danced before him. Her laughing face, so open and happy. These things and many more kept running on in his mind even after he was on his feet and walking again. She was so impulsive, so sweet and giving.

"Oh, God, how I love her! Please help me find her. I must find her!' His voice was a groan of anguish.

Carefully, Rick made his way along the path that followed through the wooded area. He decided to stay on the path and see where it would lead. As he pushed his way through the bushes, they abruptly gave way to a huge clearing. He saw the big sprawling house that stood silent as though waiting for something in the night. After finding the door locked, he used his flashlight and checked until he found an unlocked window. Pushing it open, he crawled inside and started looking around. Slowly, each room was searched. His feeling of futility grew.

Finally, he started calling to Linda, but the dark, old rooms echoed, and the stillness clearly told him that there was no one around.

When he found no sign of either girl, Rick decided to go outside. He unlocked the front door and stood on the porch for a few minutes, trying to think what he should do next. Standing there, he suddenly realized that he rain had stopped. He didn't know when, but he was very grateful that it had ended. The stars were starting to peep through the fast-moving clouds. Rick checked his watch and found that it was after midnight. He decided to walk a little farther while he waited for help to arrive. He moved to the back of the house and, as he did, he called Linda's name once more.

Linda had become exhausted trying to escape from her prison in the cramped, stuffy little shed. She had fallen asleep and was dreaming. A sweet and tender smile curled the corners of her lips. She was dreaming about Rick and she could hear him calling to her. As she tried to answer, she stirred and then slowly became aware that it was his voice. Suddenly, she was wide awake. It wasn't a dream. She could hear her wonderful Rick calling to her.

Frantic that he might pass her by and not find her, Linda started banging on the door with all her strength. She called his name over and over. She was laughing and crying, so great was her relief that she had been found.

Though it seemed to Linda to be an eternity, in only a few moments Rick was heading in the direction of her voice.

He answered her in a calm voice. "I will have you out of there in a minute, darling," he said.

He didn't feel calm though. His voice had a deep, husky quality and it was hard for him to speak. True to his word, the door swung outward and there he stood. Linda fell into his arms shaking as though she could never stop. It was the last thing she remembered for some time. Now that she was safe, the whole world slid away from her and she fainted.

XVII

The love in Rick's eyes was the last thing that Linda had seen before she fainted. When he opened the door and stood there, it had been too much for her. Rick's arms lifted her gently and his lips touched her hair as he carried her away from the musty little room. He opened the door to the house and carried Linda inside where it was dry. Sitting on the floor he held her tenderly until her eyes opened again. They sat like that for some time, with Rick's arms holding her close. They laughed even though they were both nearer to crying.

As Rick talked gently and tried to quiet the frightened girl, he said, "Linda, I could never live without you. I wouldn't even try. This night has been like a nightmare for me. I love you more than life itself."

Linda clung to him and let her fingers touch the face she loved so dearly. She would know how true his love was.

Suddenly, Rick remembered Carol.

"Did Carol close you in that shed, sweetheart," he demanded.

Linda looked so small and helpless, it made his heart ache to think of the terror she must have felt. She looked up at him, her small heart-shaped face streaked with dirt and tears.

Cuddling closer to him, she answered, "Yes, Rick, she did. She hates me. And I don't know why. I just don't understand why she did it!"

Holding her close to him, Rick told her about his marriage to Carol and how she had divorced him when he was so very ill. She had let him down when he had needed her love more than anything in the world. As Rick's story unfolded, Linda began to understand many things about Carol that had puzzled her.

With a feeling of apprehension, she asked, "Rick, where is Carol now? Did she say anything about me?"

"Carol hasn't been found yet," Rick replied slowly.

He stood up and pulled Linda to her feet. A tender kiss that told her more than any words how very worried he had been for her and how little he cared whether Carol was ever found or not.

She was a woman, fully aware, as Rick had been, that they might never have seen each other again. With his arm still around her tiny waist, Rick led her outside into the moon-bathed clearing.

"We must go down to the shore so I can give some sign that I have found you," he explained.

As they approached the small cove where he left the boat, Rick started to signal with his flashlight.

"The police will have some questions to ask," he began carefully, all the time trying to get a reply from the other shore. "It won't take long, I promise you," he smiled.

"Rick, as long as you are with me, I won't mind," Linda replied quietly. She had kept her hand clasped in his and she could not will herself to let go. She was afraid that it would turn out to be a dream and Rick would disappear again.

~ ~ ~

Uncle Edward had hurried to the house as soon as he was sure the row boat was afloat. He was still shaking his head when he reached the house. The boy had courage but on a night like this he would certainly have trouble getting to the island. It would be hard going even for a seasoned oarsman. When he walked into the house his wife's anxious face begged for good news. She knew by his haggard expression that there was none to give.

He explained what had happened without mentioning the overturned boat. He decided to wait a while in the hope he would not have to say anything about it. It would be a miracle, he felt quite sure, if the girls were to be found safe.

Aunt Susan called the police while he went up to his room to put on some dry clothes. As soon as he came down, he went to the house next door to talk to the Bensons. He wanted to be able to speak freely and not upset his wife until they had something more to go on than just the empty boat.

The Bensons were very upset. They had known the O'Connors for so long and Linda was like their own.

"We have not seen Carol since she left here this morning," they told him. "She was going to have breakfast with Linda."

Mrs. Benson mentioned that they were going to take a picnic to the island and she added that Carol seemed to be in a very happy mood.

"I do recall that," Mrs. Benson told him. "Ed, if we can help, we want to."

The three old friends headed to the O'Connor house, each one lost in thoughts of their own.

"How hard the waiting is. If only we knew something," Linda's uncle was thinking as they moved through the wet, windy yard.

They heard the police boats coming onto the beach. The police reached the O'Connor house just as Uncle Ed and the Bensons did. It was such a bad night that the men were grateful for the hot coffee that was waiting inside.

These men and their wives were friends of the O'Connors as well, and had been for many years. When something happened in their town there was no question who would help. The whole community would be there as soon as the word spread.

The wind was whistling outside, and the rain was pounding against the window. Aunt Susan tried hard not to think of Linda outside in such weather. She knew how worried her husband was and she felt she must not let him see her crying now. He was trying, just as hard, not to show how much Linda's disappearance had upset him, she was certain. To keep her hands busy, she found dry jackets so that some of the men could change from the wet ones they were wearing.

Mrs. Benson did her best to help but there wasn't much comfort to offer. With the storm raging outside, the hours were passing swiftly.

The men headed for the beach once more. This time, Uncle Edward and Mr. Benson were with them. Mr. O'Connor walked to the overturned boat. Here he explained that Rick had headed for the island with the row boat. In his heart, he was praying that the young man had made it. He could not have stopped Rick and, if he had been a little younger, nothing could have stopped Uncle Edward from going along. Rick had determination and Uncle Ed knew there would never be any doubt in the O'Connor household in the future about Rick's feeling for Linda. No man would go out on that treacherous water in a row boat on such a night unless he was willing to take a chance on being drowned. But the look on Rick's face showed no sign of fear for his own life. It was clear to Uncle Edward that he was only thinking of the girl he loved. His white head nodded in silent approval at this thought.

Aunt Susan waited for some word. She tried to talk to Mrs. Benson but the conversation kept returning to Linda. They spoke of what she had been like as a child, how she had been so anxious to start school. Her aunt talked about her graduation with deep pride in her voice. Linda has been so determined to have a career, even though she had enough money to do nothing for the rest of her life.

They had been so happy when she met a young man, fell in love, and was were married for a brief time. But he had been snatched away from her in such a harsh way. It had taken a long time for her to adjust to being a widow. She was so young; her aunt's heart had ached for her. Linda decided that a job, somewhere away from the place where she married and knew such heartache, would help her. It was with a heavy heart that her aunt and uncle watched her pack and leave the home she loved so dearly. In time, her zest for living returned and, being young, her job and her friends helped her to reach a new maturity.

"I'll never be so vulnerable again," she had promised herself.

A good many of her weekends were spent with her family and she never missed coming home for a special occasion. With the help of her friend, Sandy, she found a little apartment in New York. Even though she could have afforded a much larger one, she was happy with the one she chose. It was in the same building as Sandy's.

She was very careful to dress as casually as her friends did and she was so sweet and friendly that she soon had other friends in the building. Linda learned to live on her small salary. Her family was very proud of her and ever though they kept enough money at her disposal for whatever she might need, she left it in the bank.

Mr. and Mrs. O'Connor often visited New York and stayed with Linda. Sometimes they attended a play. Other times, they just spent quiet weekends with her. It always seemed to delight her when they came, and she would make special meals so that their visit was like a vacation. How happy they had been for Linda when they found out about Rick.

The thought of Rick brought Mrs. O'Connor back to the present with a jolt. She realized that the rain had stopped and that the wind was not blowing as hard as before. She hoped it might be a good omen.

She could hear the men out on the water shouting to one another and she knew they had not yet found the girls. The thought brought tears to her eyes again and Mrs. Benson noticed at once. She insisted that they go into the kitchen where she would make tea for them.

Mrs. Benson felt almost as badly as the O'Connors. She realized that, if her daughter had lived, perhaps she would be out there tonight. Their one little girl was their only child. They had adopted her. She had lived for only eighteen months and then died from pneumonia. It had taken a long time to adjust to the loss. Mrs. Benson's health had not been good after that so there was no talk of adoption again.

Their love and interest in Linda - and her love for them in return - had helped them through that sad time. In a small way, Linda had helped them all through the years.

She walked over to the big kitchen window and stood there looking out. The first star came blinking from behind the dark clouds. Mrs. Benson walked back to the table and sat down. They were both thinking that maybe the girls had found shelter from the rain and that now, maybe, the men would be able to find them.

After a while, the kitchen door opened, and Uncle Edward came into the room. His wife and Mrs. Benson both arose quickly form the table.

"Is there any news, Ed," his wife asked, hardly daring to hope.

He answered his wife slowly, "Rick waved his flashlight from the island, mother. I don't know what he found, but he must have found something."

Although her heart was heavy, she said, "Thank heavens Rick made it all right. He is such a wonderful boy."

"That he is, Mother," was the reply from a man who knew just how courageous Rick really was. "It took a lot of courage for him to start across that swirling water in the dark with nothing but two oars and a home-made rowboat."

Ed was talking and pouring a cup of the good hot tea that Mrs. Benson had just made. As he passed the window, he noticed that the big full moon had come out and was bathing the world with its beautiful light.

XVIII

Finally, Rick saw a flashing light answering his own signal. He and Linda sat down to wait. He knew someone would be there soon. Wearily, Linda sat in the circle of Rick's arms, her head resting on his shoulder. She began to feel hungry again. It had been such a long time since she had eaten.

By the time the boat reached them, she was too weak to get to her feet. Rick lifted her slight body into his arms and carried her aboard the large craft. No one asked any questions as they sped quickly toward the beckoning shore. There would be time enough for that later.

The beach was brightly lighted by the searchers. Many pairs of hands were there to help the tired passengers from the boat. Rick insisted on carrying Linda himself, although he was so tired he staggered slightly when he stepped onto the pier. He walked across the beach and up the stairs to the garden with his precious burden.

~ ~ ~

Uncle Ed had not told his wife much and now, he stood by the window watching to see who would come ashore. When he saw that it was Rick, with Linda in his arms, he let out a happy sigh. He would never admit, even to

166

himself, how afraid that little overturned boat had made him feel.

All night, he had tried desperately to get his wife to rest for a while. Though he had promised to wake her, she steadfastly refused. Each time he suggested it, she would say, "I must wait until Linda gets home."

Now, as footsteps approached, Uncle Edward hurried to let the weary couple in.

"Mother," he cried excitedly, "Come here! Linda is home!"

Aunt Susan came hurrying out with a happy smile which lit up her whole face. They followed Rick as he walked to the wide foyer and gently put Linda on the sofa.

In an unsteady voice he said, "Here she is — safe and sound."

Aunt Susan held her niece in her arms, with tears filling her faded eyes. Mrs. Benson joined them. She too was crying. Uncle Edward had a suspicious moisture glimmering in his faded blue eyes when he bent to kiss her forehead.

Linda tried to speak. "I am so sorry that I worried you," she began. Her voice was so low that it was barely audible.

Aunt Susan, a frown between her brows, insisted that she was going to call the family doctor.

"Please, don't call him, Aunt Susan. I am all right. Truly, I am. I am just very hungry and oh, so tired. If I could just take a bath and have some rest, I will be good as new," she promised. But she could not keep the weakness from her voice.

Rick insisted on carrying her up to her room and Linda did not put up much of an argument. The stairs did look very long to her on this cold night.

Aunt Susan and Mrs. Benson bustled right along behind them. They made Linda sit quietly while they did everything. It was finally decided that Mrs. Benson would make a tray and Aunt Susan would help Linda get bathed and into bed.

Rick was already in the bathroom running a tub of water, while Aunt Susan was busy finding a nightgown and robe. Linda could smell the delicious fragrance coming from the tub. It was so good to be here in her bright room after so many hours in that dark, musty shed. The thought of it made her shudder.

Just then, Rick walked into the room. He put his hand on her cheek as though he could read her mind.

"I'll return soon, and you had better be in bed or I will put you there myself."

Linda gave a pale imitation of her usual impish smile and, with an answering grin, Rick left the room.

Aunt Susan refused to go downstairs until her niece was ready to get into bed. She even insisted on brushing Linda's hair. Her love for her niece was in every stroke of the brush.

The tears were smarting behind Linda's eyelids again. Reaching up, she took the woman's worn hand in her own soft one.

"You and Uncle Ed have been so good to me. I love you both so very much," she said.

Aunt Susan just hugged her close for a moment saying, "I will see where that food is."

As Aunt Susan opened the door to leave, Rick came in wearing his robe and pajamas. Without a word, he lifted Linda from her chair and deposited her on the bed.

"I said you were to go straight to bed."

He tried to sound stern, but his gentle voice gave him away. Before he could remove his arms, Linda reached up and, slipping her arms tightly around his neck, she pulled his handsome head down until it was close to her.

"You know, Rick, all I could think of was, 'suppose you never found me.' I wouldn't be able to tell you how very much I love you. And, I realized for the first time, how quickly what we love can slip away."

His arms tightened around her.

"We will talk about this again someday, sweetheart, when we both have moved past the horror of it all. You are safe now and that's all I care about for the present. Something made me come home early. I don't know what - but thank God I did!"

He kissed her – a tender, lingering kiss that needed no words. They didn't even notice the O'Connors standing in the doorway.

Without a sound, Uncle Edward placed the steaming trays down on a table inside the door. The smiling couple quietly left the two young lovers alone.

There would be plenty of time to talk about tonight. The important thing was that Linda had come home safely. There was a wedding coming up soon and many plans to be made.

Rick and Linda were too preoccupied with the present to worry about anything else right now.

ABOUT THE AUTHOR

Margaret Nogan was born in Waterbury, Vermont. One of fifteen children, she began to support herself at the age of fourteen and eventually joined the army where she first began to travel around the world. Retiring from the military she competed her education at the University of Vermont, married and had two children. For more than 20 years she had a successful second career as a realtor. In 1955 she was awarded publication of the poem which appears at the beginning of this book.

All her life, Margaret wanted to find the time to be a full-time writer. But her life was brimming over with seven grandchildren and twelve great grandchildren, and with travelling, painting and quilting.

Now, happily living in historic Newark, Delaware, where she still enjoys all these diversions, she is finally ready to begin publishing some of her works.

At the age of ninety-one, Margaret walks more than a mile every day and she does to briskly with no assistance needed or wanted! This, her first novel, is only the beginning of what is destined to become a new, thrilling and adventurous contribution to the literary world.

Made in the USA
Middletown, DE
06 May 2018